WIRE
MAGIC

WIRE
MAGIC

MICHAEL BALL

NORTH LIGHT BOOKS
Cincinnati, Ohio

First published in North America
in 2000 by North Light Books
an imprint of F&W Publications, Inc.
1507 Dana Avenue
Cincinnati, OH 45207
1-800/289-0963

ISBN 1-58180-089-4

Managing Editor: Coral Walker
Project Editor: Gillian Haslam
Assistant Editor: Kate Latham
Design and Art Direction: Blackjacks
Production: Caroline Hansell
Photographer: Emma Peios
Illustrator: Ian Sidaway

2 4 6 8 10 9 7 5 3 1

Reproduction by Modern Age Repro House Ltd, Hong Kong
Printed and bound in Singapore by Tien Wah Press (Pte) Ltd

IMPORTANT

DISCLAIMER

ACKNOWLEDGMENTS

Thanks to: Coral Walker for making this book a pleasure to write, and the design and photography team – Jack Buchan and Emma Peios. Also thanks to Kate Latham, Alice Bell and Gillian Haslam at New Holland, Angie and Paul Boyer at *The Craftsman Magazine* in the UK (+44 (0)1377 255213) and Michael Freeman and Mark Dale at Freedale Press in Maidstone.

Most importantly, my thanks go to Angela Ball, Debbie Siniska, Victoria Salter and Janine Baxter.

CONTENTS

INTRODUCTION

Wirework is one of those rare crafts where it's possible to make functional and good-looking items that you will want to have around your home without needing a lot of equipment. A pair of round-nose pliers, a pair of straight-nose pliers and a pair of strong wire cutters are sufficient for the majority of wirework projects.

Wire is not a new material: it's an ancient one that has been rendered commonplace by technology. It's hard to imagine how amazing wire must have seemed when wire was formed by hand. Long ingots were pulled through a series of holes in a sheet of hard metal until the ingot was turned into a thread of metal.

When wire production was mechanized during the nineteenth century many kinds of inexpensive wire became readily available. Black annealed iron wire was used to make a vast range of household items from baskets and containers of all kinds to candleholders and letter racks, but throughout the twentieth century many of these items were replaced by moulded plastic products.

In recent years wirework has experienced a resurgence of interest amongst artists, craftspeople and makers. This is due to the genuine versatility of wire and the willingness of craftspeople to combine new materials with traditional techniques. Techniques from crafts as diverse as wickerwork, coppice fence-making and textile-weaving can all be applied to wirework with innovative results.

If you have never tried wirework before, I hope this book will make you want to pick up a pair of pliers and have a go. The projects range from simple items, such as the leaf wall hooks on page 16, which are suitable for absolute beginners, to advanced projects like the more intricate fish griller on page 58. These projects are interspersed with a series of gallery sections featuring original and inspirational designs by wireworkers from around the world.

Michael Ball

Wirework animals
by Tasuku Gouda

MATERIALS & EQUIPMENT

The following list describes the equipment used in wirework. As mentioned on page 6, you will find that you can begin this craft with a very small range of tools and, therefore, minimum outlay. Only four of the projects in this book require soldering, so there are still plenty of projects to choose from if you do not wish to buy soldering equipment.

EQUIPMENT

Round-nose pliers: These have round jaws which taper along their length and are one of the most useful tools for wirework.

Ring bending pliers: These serve the same function as round-nose pliers, but are better suited to bending thicker wire.

Straight-nose pliers: Straight-nose pliers have smooth straight jaws. Snipe-nose pliers are similar but usually have serrated jaws which will mark soft wire such as copper or aluminium.

Household pliers: Household pliers have straight jaws which are toothed so they can grip firmly. They usually have a pair of wire cutters built-in, and sometimes have a second cutter for thick wire on the side of one jaw next to the pivot.

Vise grips: Vise grips have jaws which can be set so they will lock closed. This locking action can be particularly useful when working with large diameter wire, when the grips can be used as a movable handle which can be fixed in place at any point along the length of a wire. A lever positioned inside one of the handles releases the locking action.

Parallel pliers: Most pliers open and close like a pair of scissors, but with parallel pliers the jaws move parallel to one another, which means that the jaws grip equally well along their whole length. The most commonly used parallel pliers are straight-nose.

Wire cutters: Wire cutters have hardened, tempered steel jaws and are available in various sizes. End-cutters, which have their cutting edges positioned at right-angles to the handles, are also available and can be useful.

Bolt cutters: Bolt cutters are ideal for cutting wire which is too large or too hard to be cut with wire cutters. Wire cutters are sufficient for the majority of projects in this book.

Soldering iron: You need a 75-watt or 100-watt soldering iron. Smaller wattage irons such as those used for electrical work tend to cool down too quickly. I use a 75-watt soldering iron designed for stained glass work which is ideal.

Solder: I use 50/50 tin-lead solder with a liquid safety flux which is applied with a brush. Electrical solder which has the flux built-in works just as well, but can be more expensive.

Protective gloves and safety spectacles: Cotton-backed leather gloves are a worthwhile investment. It's also worth having a pair of plastic safety spectacles, particularly when stretching wire and working with heavy-gauge wire.

Pens: Permanent markers and OHP (overhead projector) pens, can be used to draw lines onto wire. OHP pens have a thinner nib than permanent markers, but the ink from both pens stays on the wire, rather than transferring onto your fingers.

STRAIGHT-NOSE
PLIERS

ROUND-NOSE
PLIERS

RING BENDING
PLIERS

HOUSEHOLD
PLIERS

PARALLEL PLIERS

PALM GRIP
WIRE CUTTERS

SAFETY
SPECTACLES

WIRE CUTTERS

BOLT
CUTTERS

SOLDER

AWL

PROTECTIVE GLOVES

SOLDERING IRON

VISE GRIPS

PERMANENT MARKER PEN

TAPE MEASURE

OHP (OVERHEAD
PROJECTOR) PEN

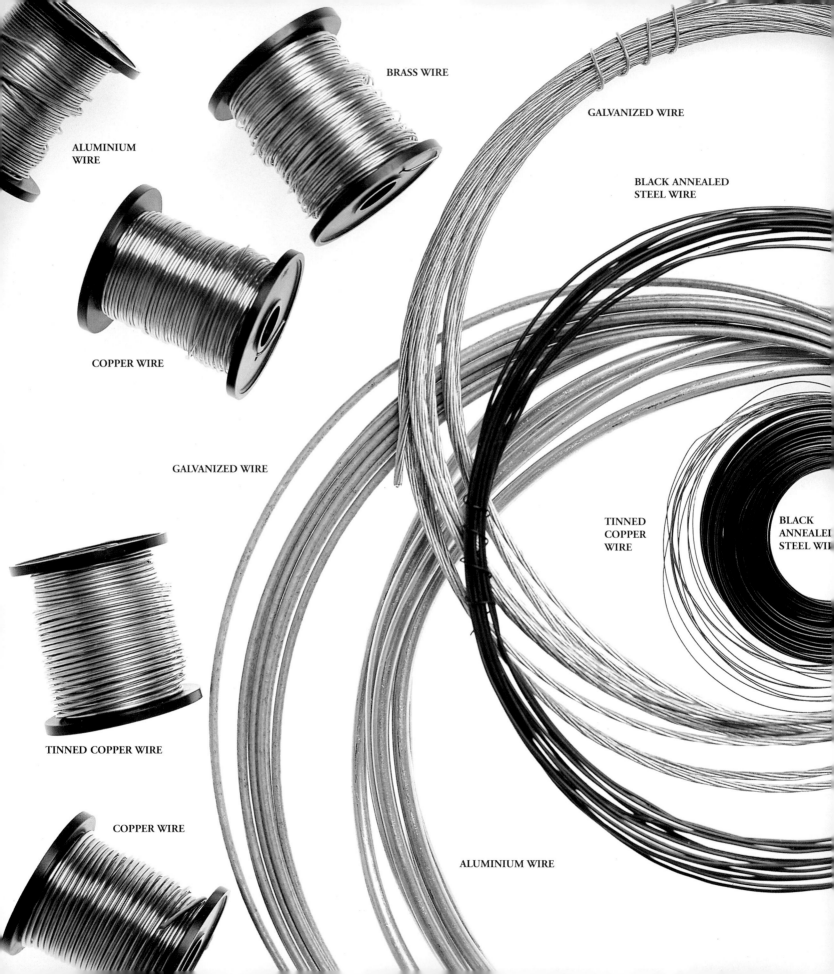

ALUMINIUM
WIRE

BRASS WIRE

GALVANIZED WIRE

BLACK ANNEALED
STEEL WIRE

COPPER WIRE

GALVANIZED WIRE

TINNED
COPPER
WIRE

BLACK
ANNEALED
STEEL WIRE

TINNED COPPER WIRE

COPPER WIRE

ALUMINIUM WIRE

MATERIALS

Wire gauges: Wire tends to be measured either in millimetres or by the Standard Wire Gauge (SWG) system. You will find that black annealed steel wire is nearly always sold by gauge. Here is a conversion table to show the relation of mm to Standard Wire Gauge:

mm	SWG	mm	SWG	mm	SWG	mm	SWG
4.000	8	1.000	19	0.315	30	0.125	40
3.250	10	0.900	20	0.280	31	0.112	41
3.000	11	0.800	21	0.265	32	0.100	42
2.650	12	0.710	22	0.250	33	0.090	43
2.360	13	0.630	23	0.236	34	0.080	44
2.000	14	0.560	24	0.212	35	0.071	45
1.800	15	0.500	25	0.200	36	0.060	46
1.600	16	0.450	26	0.170	37	0.050	47
1.400	17	0.400	27	0.150	38	0.040	48
1.250	18	0.375	28	0.132	39	0.025	50

Aluminium: Annealed aluminium wire is very soft and easy to work with, and wire as thick as 6 mm (¼ in) in diameter can be bent by hand. Aluminium has a high resistance to corrosion, and so is ideal for making kitchenware.

Brass: Brass is an alloy or blend of zinc and copper. It is harder than copper, and when polished it has a colour similar to 9k gold. Brass tarnishes to a soft brown.

Copper: Copper wire is perhaps the most versatile wire to work with. It is very malleable (you can bend it repeatedly in the same place without the metal cracking) which makes it very well suited for most wirework projects. It is used extensively for electrical cables, and good quality wire can be reclaimed from old household wiring. Tin-plated, silver-plated and coloured enamel-plated copper wire can be bought from beadwork and electrical wire suppliers. It can be patinated to a natural blue-green finish.

Steel: Black annealed mild steel wire is easy to work with. Because the wire will rust naturally, it is worth applying a sealant over completed pieces that are designed to be used outdoors. The size of this wire is specified by gauge.

Galvanized wire: Galvanized steel wire is used extensively for fencing and gardening wire. It is strong and has a corrosion-resistant zinc plating.

Wire mesh: Wire mesh is available in a broad range of different types, from square woven meshes to expanded aluminium mesh and galvanized chicken wire. Meshes come in a wide range of different metals, including brass, stainless steel and copper.

SURFACE FINISHES

Paint: Most wire (except zinc-plated wire) can be easily painted with acrylic spray. Apply the spray in several thin coats for a good finish, allowing the coats to dry between applications.

Patina finishes: If you expose copper or steel to the elements for long enough, they will oxidize or patinate. Steel will rust, and copper will turn blue or green. Patina finishes allow you to speed up the process to just a few hours.

BASIC TECHNIQUES

'Whatever you can do or dream you can, begin it. Boldness has genius, power and magic in it.' – Goethe

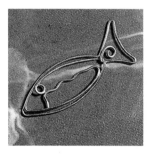

The best way to learn about wirework is to start making something. Begin with something small and simple, firstly because you are more likely to achieve good results and gain confidence, and also because the attention to detail that you develop from working with small things will pay dividends when you make larger items. Paperclips and bookmarks (see left) are a good first project – make your own designs or copy the templates on page 78. All you will need is a pair of straight-nose pliers, a pair of round-nose pliers and a pair of fine wire cutters.

BENDING WIRE

Although everyone finds the techniques that best suit them and there isn't usually a right or wrong way to do it, if you're starting wirework it can be easy to make life unnecessarily difficult for yourself by the way that you use a pair of pliers. Surely, you're thinking, you simply pick up the pliers and bend the wire with them and that's an end to the matter. Not entirely.

If you hold the wire still and rotate your wrist in order to bend the wire, all of the strain of bending is on your wrist, and when using a thick piece of wire, it can be quite a considerable strain. In many cases it's preferable to keep the pliers still and pull the end of the wire round with your other hand. This way the pliers define the point at which the wire will bend and you are free to apply the strength of your whole arm, which usually makes the process much easier.

With very thick pieces of wire, it is often a good idea to use vise grips which can be set so that they lock onto a piece of wire, leaving you free to focus on bending the wire without having to worry about the pliers slipping.

BENDING WIRE

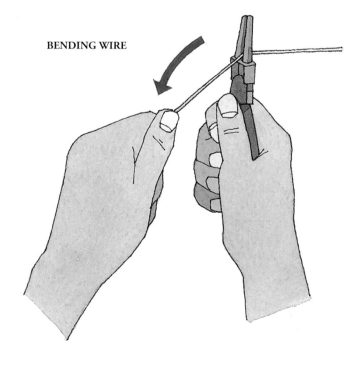

BINDING

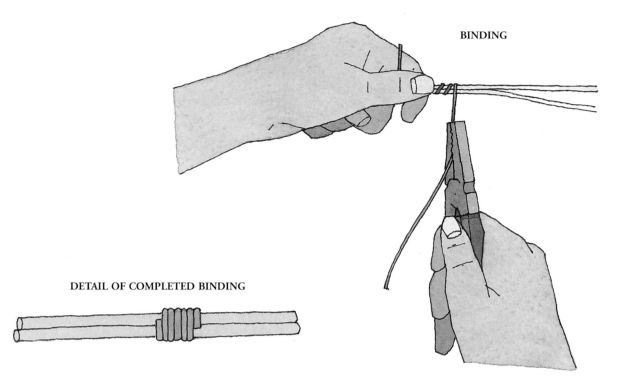

DETAIL OF COMPLETED BINDING

BINDING

One of the simplest ways to join two pieces of wire is to bind them together with a thinner wire. It's often a good idea to make a series of light indentations with a pair of wire cutters in the wires to be joined to prevent the binding wire slipping. Take a couple of open turns around the wires to hold them tightly before starting to bend the close turns of the bindings (see large illustration above). Pull the wire tight with a pair of straight-nose pliers, then trim off the excess wire and press down the end so that it lies flat. The detail above shows the completed binding with the open diagonal turns trimmed off.

Continuous binding: If you have a series of joins to be made along the same wire, it makes sense to join them all with one continuous binding instead of using lots of short lengths. In some projects in this book (such as on the trunk of the Christmas tree on page 24), continuous binding is applied without a gap between each turn, but it's more common to apply binding, with a gap between each turn, like the one shown in the illustration on the right. To finish off, apply two or more close turns before cutting off any excess wire.

Temporary binding: The idea of temporary binding is to hold the pieces of a wirework structure in place so that they won't slide or move while the permanent bindings are being applied. Use short pieces of wire or garden ties for temporary bindings.

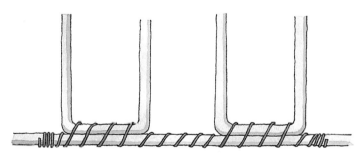

CONTINUOUS BINDING

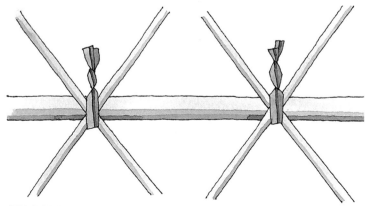

TEMPORARY BINDING

LINKING LOOPS

This technique provides a very strong join. It's useful for making circles or any other shape where the ends meet. First of all, bend the wire upwards at about 45 degrees, 2½ cm (1 in) from the end. Now bend the end down into a loop. Repeat this for the other end, but this time bend the wire laterally to form a loop at right angles to the first. Trim off excess wire and link the loops together. Crimp them closed with a pair of vise grips (or household pliers).

LINKING LOOPS

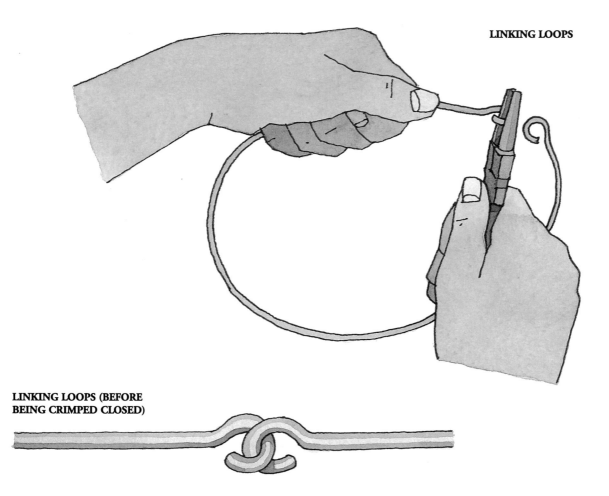

LINKING LOOPS (BEFORE BEING CRIMPED CLOSED)

STRAIGHTENING WIRE

Soft wire can often be straightened very easily by stretching it. This technique works particularly well with ordinary annealed copper wire, which is great if you plan to recycle copper cabling. First of all, untangle the wire – don't bother about any kinks, just make sure the cable isn't actually knotted anywhere. Enlist an assistant bearing vise grips (or household pliers). Grip the other end with a pair of vise grips and pull! You should both wear safety spectacles and protective gloves just in case the wire should break. It's amazing to see a tangle of wire turned into a perfectly straight length by this technique.

TWISTING WIRE

Twisted wire, made from two or more strands twisted together, is often used for its decorative qualities, but its strength can also be an advantage. To make a 2-ply twist, cut a length of wire and bend it back on itself in the middle to make a loop. Allow more wire than you think you need as the wire will become shorter during the twisting process. Always wear eye protection, such as safety spectacles, and protective gloves – although I've never known it to happen, there's always a chance that the wire may snap.

Fix the loop in position around a wall hook, then grip the two ends with a pair of vise grips. Ensure that the vise grips are properly adjusted so that the wire is firmly held. Pull and turn the vise grips at the same time until the wire is evenly twisted along its whole length. If twisting thin wire, you can fit the two ends in the chuck of a hand drill and simply turn the handle.

SOLDERING

Soldering is a permanent and simple way to join copper, tin and galvanized (zinc-plated) steel. Although it can take a little practice to achieve smooth, neat solder joints, it is a useful technique to master.

You will need a 75- or 100-watt soldering iron and solder. I use 50/50 tin-lead solder which comes in 4 mm (³⁄₁₆ in) rods and is available from stained glass suppliers. Always wash your hands after working with solder and work in a well-ventilated area – remember that solder contains lead. You will also need a heat-proof board and some safety flux. Flux removes any oxidation on the surface of the metal and improves the solder flow. It is usually sold as a blue liquid which is applied with a small brush. Always wear safety spectacles when working with solder.

Brush some safety flux over the area to be soldered. Press the tip of the soldering iron onto the area to heat up the wires. Melt a small amount of solder onto the tip of the soldering iron and hold the iron with the tip and the molten solder touching the wires until the solder flows. If the solder won't flow or flows unevenly, apply more flux and re-apply the solder.

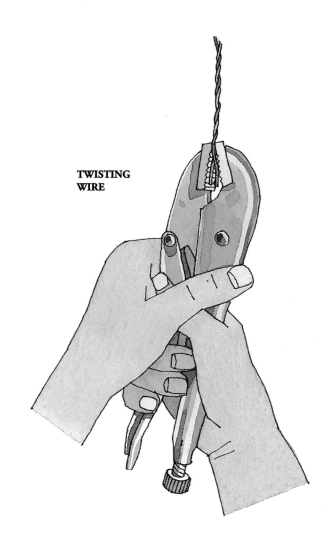

TWISTING WIRE

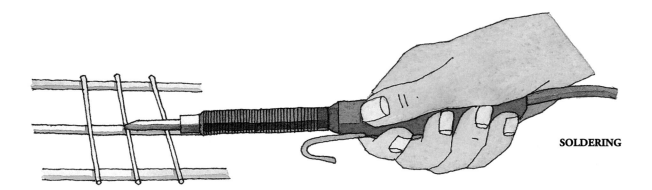

SOLDERING

LEAF WALL HOOKS

These simple wall hooks, made from soft copper wire, are a good project to practise basic bending skills and are ideal for beginners.

YOU WILL NEED:

56 cm (22 in) of 2 mm copper wire
Wire cutters
Round-nose pliers or ring bending pliers
OHP pen
Vise grips
Bolt cutters
Approximately 15 cm (6 in) of 1 mm copper wire

BENDING THE LEAF SHAPE

1 Photocopy the template on page 77. Cut a 56 cm (22 in) length of 2 mm wire. Following the template starting from the end marked with a star on the template, use round-nose or ring bending pliers to bend the wire. Check your work against the template at regular intervals. When you come to the first tight loop, bend the wire up to the middle of the loop, then mark this point with an OHP pen. The end of the wire should go under the curve you've just bent. Bend the wire loosely round and close the loop up by pressing on either side with the vise grips as shown (fig. 1). Continue bending the wire following the template until you reach the apex of the leaf shape. From this point on the end should go over the curve of each loop.

2 When the leaf shape is complete, you will be left with a length of wire for the hook section. Straighten this section of wire. Bend the wire back on itself after 5 cm (2 in). Use the vise grips to close the loop.

BENDING THE HOOK SECTION

3 Bend the loop for the screw fixing on the top of the doubled wire and trim off any excess. Bend the loop that will be the end of the hook gently downwards about 1 cm (⅜ in) from the end. Make the bend to form the hook about 3 cm (1¼ in) back from the loop (fig. 2).

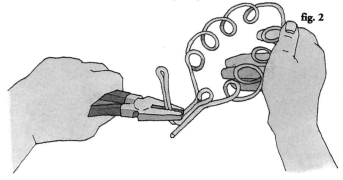

fig. 2

4 Use a pair of bolt cutters to provide a key just below the base of the leaf. The 2.5 cm (1 in) section of wire that was the starting point for this project fits behind the doubled wire that forms the hook. Bend it so that it follows the curve of the loop. Bind with 1 mm copper wire, cutting the ends so that they tuck neatly behind the hook.

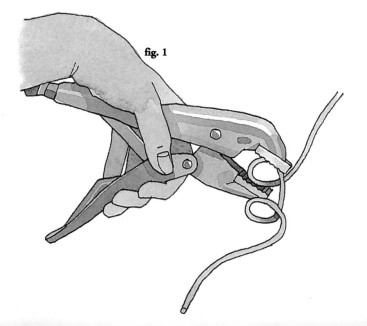

fig. 1

FRUIT BOWL

This fruit bowl is surprisingly strong considering that it uses a minimum amount of wire. When you've finished making it, wipe over the wires with a cloth dipped in a little olive oil to protect the surface from rust.

YOU WILL NEED:

Approximately 8 m (26 ft 3 in) of 1.6 mm (16 gauge)
   black annealed steel wire
Wire cutters
Straight-nose pliers
Vise grips

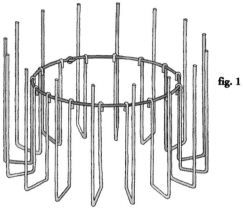

fig. 1

MAKING THE TOP AND BOTTOM CIRCLES

1 Cut a 91 cm (36 in) length of wire and bend it into a circle. Form a pair of linking loops 2.5 cm (1 in) from each end, bending one loop vertically and one loop horizontally so they will lock together. Link the loops and trim back the ends to 6 mm (¼ in) long. Crimp the loops closed with vise grips.

2 Form the bottom circle from a 15 cm (6 in) length of wire. Bend the ends back 2.5 cm (1 in) from each end as before to make two loops. Trim off the excess wire but don't link the loops together at this stage.

3 Make two marks directly opposite each other on the top circle. A light indentation made with a pair of wire cutters will show up better than a pen mark on this dark-coloured wire. Now sub-divide the two sections to give a mark at each quarter. Continue this process until there are 16 equally-spaced divisions around the circle.

ADDING THE RADIAL WIRES

4 Cut a 40 cm (16 in) length of wire. Straighten the wire and form a loop 2.5 cm (1 in) from one end. Trim the excess wire back to 6 mm (¼ in). Hook the loop at the end of the wire over the top circle with the hooked section of the loop on the

inside of the circle. Line the loop up with one of the marks on the circle and crimp it closed with vise grips. Cut 15 more 40 cm (16 in) lengths of wire and repeat the process until you have one radial wire linked at each point around the circle.

5 Bend each radial wire outwards away from the circle at a right angle 15 cm (6 in) down from the loop. Make a second right angle 5 cm (2 in) further from this point, bending the wires so that the ends point upwards (fig. 1).

6 Thread the bottom circle around the 16 radial wires at the first right angle. Link the loops in the bottom circle and crimp closed. Use your hands to curve each radial wire gently between the top loop and the first right angle where it meets the bottom circle. Use vise grips to crimp this right angle into a loop on each radial wire, locking the bottom circle in place (see fig. 2).

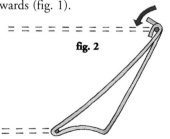

fig. 2

7 Bend the end of each radial wire over into a third right angle 12.5 cm (5 in) from the second one and bend the end over the top of the large circle to form a loop. Trim the end off as usual to 6 mm (¼ in) and crimp each loop closed (fig. 2).

BOWLS & BASKETS

1
Woven circular bowl
(Wendy Abrahams)

2
Fruit bowl
(Mia Agnesson)

3
Oval bowl
(Wendy Abrahams)

4
Peacock bowl
(Wendy Abrahams)

LETTER RACK

This letter rack is made from a series of simple modular units – you can add as few or as many sections as you wish. If you have them, ring bending pliers are useful for this project as they make it easier to bend the wire without marking it.

YOU WILL NEED:

Approximately 3.5 m (11½ ft) of 1.6 mm (16 gauge) black annealed steel wire
Wire cutters
Round-nose or ring bending pliers
Vise grips or household pliers

fig. 1

fig. 2

BENDING THE WIRE

1 Cut a 40 cm (16 in) length of wire and straighten it. Using the main unit template on page 75 as a guide, start bending the first curve about 7.5 cm (3 in) from the end of the wire using round-nose or ring bending pliers. Then grip the wire at the first point where the pattern doubles back on itself and pull the wire into a tight 'U' shape. You will probably find it hard to bend the recurve as tightly as shown in the design: to tighten it, press each side of the curve with vise grips or household pliers. Bend the wire to follow the design, repeating this process at each tight corner. You will be left with a second end approximately 7.5 cm (3 in) in length. Repeat this whole step until you have made seven of the basic shapes.

2 Three of the shapes will make up the top units – these each have one of the top wires bent into a hanging loop. Following the loop template on page 75, take a main unit and bend the vertical left-hand end at a right angle to the left at a point 7.5 cm (3 in) from the end. Bend it round into a double circle and trim off the excess wire. Cut the right-hand end off at a point 5 cm (2 in) from the end and thread it through the double circle. Bend the end over to form a loop. Cut off the excess and crimp the loop with vise grips or household pliers to lock the wire in place (fig. 1).

3 Bend the ends of the remaining shapes into a 'Y' shape using the template as a guide. Bend a loop at each end and thread them through the lower curves of the shape above them. Cut the ends back leaving about 6 mm (¼ in) for the loop and crimp it closed with vise grips or household pliers.

4 The three lower shapes each have an additional fixing point added. Cut a 10 cm (4 in) length of wire. Bend a loop in the middle of the wire and form a hanging loop at each end (see template). Thread the ends through the lower curves, trim back to 6 mm (¼ in) and crimp to close.

CHRISTMAS TREE

This tiny freestanding Christmas tree is made from only four lengths of wire – the branches and star are made from two lengths, the circle at the base uses another length and the thin wire which binds the trunk section makes the fourth.

YOU WILL NEED:

Approximately 2.5 m (8 ft 2 in) of 0.56 mm (24 gauge) black annealed steel wire
Wire cutters
Vise grips
Matchstick
Round-nose pliers
Straight-nose pliers
Approximately 1 m (39 in) of 0.4 mm (27 gauge) black annealed steel wire

THE WIRE

1 Enlarge the templates on page 75. Cut a 1 m (39 in) length of 0.56 mm wire. Mark the centre point of the wire and bend a star starting from this point, following the straight-branched template. Then bend the three straight branches on either side – each branch is a long, flattened loop. Bend the wire at both ends to form a 'root' on each side which will lock onto the base circle. Cut off any excess wire.

2 Cut another 1 m (39 in) length of 0.56 mm wire and bend it in half. This wire is bent in the same way as in step 1 except that this time you omit the star and start bending from the top of the trunk.

fig. 1

TWISTING THE WIRE

3 Adjust a pair of vise grips to clamp around the wires. Grip the wires for each branch where they leave the main trunk and insert a matchstick in the loop at the end of the branch. Pull the wire tight and twist the matchstick until the wire is evenly twisted (fig. 1). Repeat for each branch in turn, as well as the 'root' sections. Using round-nose pliers, bend each branch into a spiral following the template.

BINDING THE SECTIONS TOGETHER

4 Fit the two pieces together perpendicular to one another, with the top of the second section located at the bottom of the star on the first section (see fig. 2). Temporarily bind the two pieces together at several points down the trunk. Cut an 80 cm (31 in) length of 0.4 mm wire and bind the entire length of the trunk tightly, starting just below the star. Use straight-nose pliers to pull the wire tight as you bind. If the branches get in the way, bend them out of the way while you bind around them, then bend them back into position.

fig. 2

5 Bend a circle for the base from 0.56 mm wire using the template as a guide. Bend the ends back and form them into locking loops. Thread one end through each of the loops on the end of the four 'roots', then crimp the locking loops together to complete the circle.

WALL CLOCK

This clock combines brass foil with thin sheet metal cut from a cookie tin lid. Thin tin-plated steel can usually be cut fairly easily with a pair of heavy duty craft snips, but you could use a pair of tin snips instead.

YOU WILL NEED:

15 cm (6 in) square of tin plate (cut from a cookie tin lid)
Sheet of carbon paper
Ball-point pen
Protective leather gloves
Multi-purpose craft cutters or tin snips
Drill or hammer and nail
Piece of scrap wood
10 sq cm (4 sq in) brass embossing foil
Heavy-duty craft knife
Clock mechanism and hands
Superglue (cyano-acrylate adhesive)
Approximately 5 m (16 ft 5 in) of 1 mm soft brass wire
Safety spectacles
Household pliers or vise grips
Hand drill
Masking tape
OHP pen
Garden twist ties
Approximately 1 m (39 in) stranded brass picture wire
Wire cutters
Glue gun or strong glue such as epoxy resin

MAKING THE METAL STAR AND CIRCLE

1 Enlarge the templates on page 74. The main template shows the connections as you will see them when looking at the back of the clock. Lay the star design over the tin plate. Put the carbon paper between the template and the tin and transfer the design by pressing over the lines with a ball-point pen.

2 Wearing protective gloves, cut out the star – I used a pair of multi-purpose craft cutters, which look like a pair of short scissors with serrated edges, but a pair of tin snips is just as good. Cut off the points of the star to make it safer.

3 The hole in the centre can either be drilled, or punched out by making a series of holes with a nail and hammer. Lay the tin plate over a piece of scrap wood while you make the hole.

4 Take the enlarged circle design and transfer it to the foil. You don't need the carbon paper as this is much thinner than tin plate – just lay the foil on a soft surface such as a newspaper and go over the lines with a ball-point pen to impress the circle into the foil. Cut out the circle and make the hole in the centre with a heavy-duty craft knife.

5 Lay the star over the circle and temporarily fit the clock mechanism into place to ensure that the holes in the star and circle line up correctly. Remove the clock mechanism and apply a small amount of superglue around the hole in the brass circle. Press the star into place and hold the two pieces together for about a minute to ensure that they are firmly fixed.

MAKING THE WIRE CIRCLE AND STAR

6 Cut a 4 m (13 ft 1 in) length of soft brass wire and fold it in half. Fix the halfway point around a fixed object such as a wall hook, or have someone grip this point firmly with household pliers or vise grips. Put on safety spectacles and leather gloves. Then fix the two ends in a hand drill, pull until the wire is taut and twist until the two strands are evenly twisted. Remove the ends from the drill.

7 Cut an 80 cm (31 in) length of the twisted wire and bend it into a circle using the large template on page 74 as a guide. The easiest way to do this is to wrap the wire around a circular object such as a bowl – choose one smaller than the circle that you want to end up with as the wire will spring back slightly. Lay the wire over the template and tape it in place with five or six pieces of masking tape (the ends will overlap).

8 Mark a joining point for the circle on one of the twisted wires in each pair with an OHP pen (fig. 1). Cut one wire

fig. 1

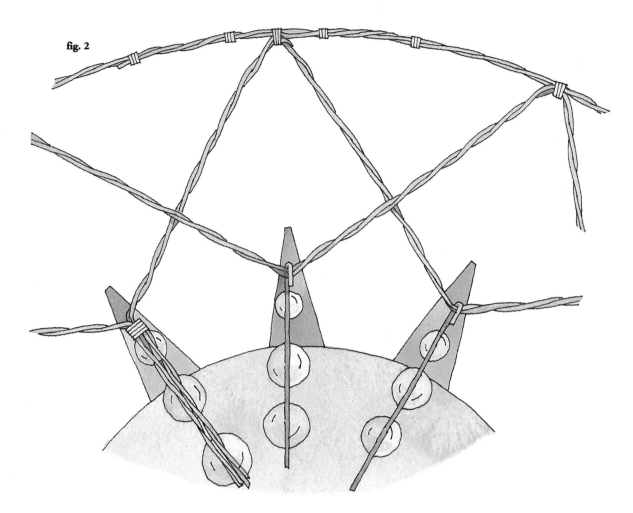

fig. 2

within each pair back to this point with a pair of fine wire cutters (you should be able to cut just one of the wires without unravelling them). With the cut wire ends level, cut the remaining two long ends back so that each one is about 2.5 cm (1 in) longer than the joining point and twist them along the circle. Remove the wire from the template and bind the ends in place with a single strand of wire cut from a length of stranded brass picture wire. Use a pair of flat-nosed pliers to pull the wire tight as you bind (you'll end up with a much stronger join this way).

9 The wire star shape is actually two separate six-pointed stars laid on top of one another. Bend these using the template as a guide. Cut the twisted ends to about 5 cm (2 in) long. These ends form linking wires to the back of the metal star on two adjacent points (as shown on the template). Tape the two stars and the circle to the template. Temporarily bind the points of the stars to the circle – garden twist ties are a quick and convenient way to do this. Cut short strands from a length of picture wire and permanently bind each point in place around the circumference of the circle. Remove the temporary ties as you work.

PUTTING IT ALL TOGETHER

10 Cut ten 6 cm (2¼ in) linking wires from plain 1 mm brass wire and join each to one of the remaining inside points of the pair of stars by making a simple loop on the end of each wire and crimping it in place. Lay the metal star and foil circle with the circle uppermost over the template and lay the wire surround in place over this. Each of the linking wires should lie along one of the points of the metal star. Fix all twelve linking wires temporarily in position with masking tape. Apply tape to every other wire. The easiest ways to bond the wires in position is to use a glue gun. Epoxy adhesive is just as good, but takes a little longer to dry. Glue the wires that are not taped in position. When the glue has dried, remove the tape and apply glue to the remaining points (fig. 2).

11 Fix the clock mechanism permanently in place (most come with a hollow screw which fixes through the hole in the centre) and fit the hands in place. Depending on the kind of mechanism, these will either push into place or have a small nut to hold them in position.

CANDLE HOLDERS

The wire petals on these candle holders can be bent to a flat design or they can be folded upwards. The petals pivot on a circular wire and interlock, so when you move one petal they all move. The centre of each candle holder is made from the base of an aluminium drinks can.

YOU WILL NEED:

Aluminium drinks can (one for each candle holder)
OHP pen
Matchbox
Protective leather gloves
Scissors
Medium sandpaper (120 grit) or steel wool
Leatherwork hole punch (2 mm [1⁄16 in] or similar)
Approximately 2.4 m (8 ft) of 1.25 mm (18 gauge) of black annealed steel wire
Approximately 25 cm (10 in) of 1.6 mm (16 gauge) of black annealed steel wire
25 cm (10 in) of 0.56 mm (24 gauge) black annealed steel wire
Vise grips
Straight-nose pliers

CUTTING THE DRINKS CAN

1 Draw a line around the drinks can about 2 cm (¾ in) from the bottom. The easiest way to do this is to use an OHP pen taped to the top of a matchbox. Place the pen on top of the matchbox on a flat surface with the nib in contact with the can. Rotate the can to make an even line all the way around.

2 Wearing protective gloves, make a hole near the top of the can with scissors. Cut down from this point and carefully around the line to remove the base of the can. Remove all the paint from the base of the can with sandpaper or steel wool.

3 Use a leatherwork hole punch to make a series of 16 holes about 1 cm (⅜ in) from the cut edge of the can using the template on page 73 as a guide. (I used a 2 mm (1⁄16 in) punch, but the size really isn't important.)

CUTTING AND BENDING THE WIRE

4 Enlarge the template on page 73. Your drinks can should be roughly the same size as the circle in the middle of the template – if it isn't, enlarge or reduce the template as necessary. Cut a 20 cm (8 in) length of 1.25 mm (18 gauge) black annealed steel wire. Bend the wire in half into a 'V' shaped 'petal' using the template as a guide. Make a mark near each end of the wire, 7.5 cm (3 in) from the point of the 'V'. Bend the wire back on itself at this point to form a loop on each end – don't close these loops yet as they will be threaded onto the main wire circle (see fig. 1). Trim the ends back to about 6 mm (¼ in). Repeat this to make a total of 12 petals.

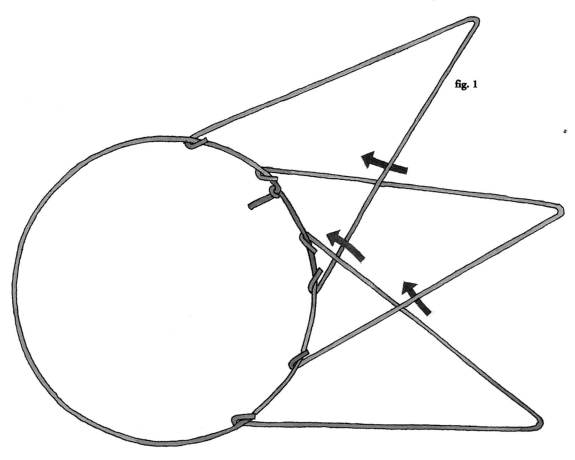

fig. 1

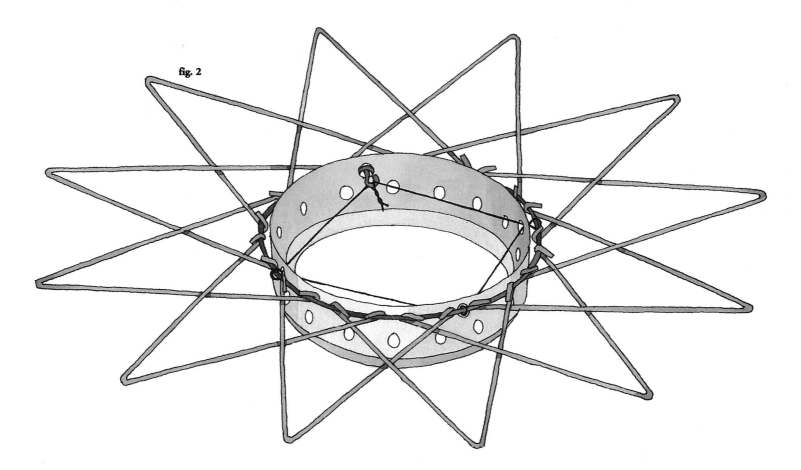

fig. 2

5 Bend a circle of 1.6 mm (16 gauge) wire to fit around the outside of the drinks can using the template as a guide. Make a bend about 2.5 cm (1 in) from one end, so that the end points inwards towards the centre of the circle. Mark the point where the straight end overlaps this inward-pointing end and bend a loop. Trim off any excess wire and crimp the loop closed with a pair of vise grips to complete the circle.

ATTACHING THE PETALS

6 Thread both of the hanging loops on the ends of one wire petal onto the circle, with the loop ends on top of the wire circle (see fig. 1). Don't try to put the petals on in an upright position, at this stage they should lie flat. Working round the circle, thread on the next petal. The right-hand end of this petal should go under the left-hand end of the first petal. Thread on the next petal – again the right-hand end of this petal should go under the left-hand end of the previous petal, but this time the right-hand end should also go over the left-hand end of the first petal (fig. 1). Continue until all the petals are in place. Crimp the loops closed

with the vise grips so that the petals cannot slip off the circle, but not so tightly that they are unable to pivot on the wire circle.

7 Make a series of four equally-spaced holes around the can with the hole punch. Each hole should be about 3 mm (⅛ in) below the cut rim. Push the inward-pointing end of the circle through one of the holes. Bend a loop on the end of this wire. Cut a 25 cm (9¾ in) length of 0.56 mm (24 gauge) wire. Thread about 2.5 cm (1 in) of this wire though the loop in the end of the circle and twist the wire with straight-nose pliers to lock it in place. Thread the other end of the wire through the next of the four holes, around the wire circle and back through the hole. Proceed until the circle wire is held firmly in place against the can. End by threading the wire through the loop where it started and twisting to lock it in place (fig. 2).

8 Gently bend the petals upwards to whatever position you wish – they should move fairly freely. Repeat these instructions to make as many more candleholders as you want. You can display some with their petals flat, and others with their petals upright (as shown on page 29).

GIFTS & ACCESSORIES

1

Recycled wire hat
(Alison Bailey Smith)

2

Feather bowls
(Wendy Abrahams)

3

Minaret boxes
(Sophie Jonas)

4

Casket box
(Sophie Jonas)

5

Titania crown
(Sophie Jonas)

SOAPDISH

I've always been fascinated by old wooden boats — I think their clean, fluid lines often have an almost organic quality about them, as if their design were based on some sort of tropical fruit. This soapdish was inspired by a blueprint of a traditional clinker-built wooden ship.

YOU WILL NEED:

Approximately 2.5 m (8 ft 2 in) of
2.5 mm tinned copper wire
40 cm (16 in) of 1 mm tinned
copper wire
Round-nose or ring bending pliers
Straight-nose pliers
Wire cutters

MAKING THE RIBS OF THE SOAPDISH

1 Enlarge the templates on page 73. There are three sections to this soapdish: the ribs of the boat, which are formed from one continuous length of wire; the backbone and the stand. Cut a 160 cm (63 in) length of the 2.5 mm wire and, using the template as a guide, bend the ribs using round-nose or ring bending pliers for the curves and straight-nose pliers at both ends. To save marking the wire with the pliers, use your hands to bend the wire wherever you can. Cut off any excess wire at the end and press out the flat shape to form the three-dimensional boat shape.

MAKING THE BACKBONE

2 Cut a 30 cm (12 in) length of 2.5 mm wire and bend the backbone section, including the loops at the ends of the wire, using the template as a guide. To make sure the ribs fit inside the curve of the backbone, it is necessary to curve the wire at the points marked with a star on the template. Check that the ribs will fit neatly together with the backbone and apply temporary bindings to hold the pieces together (fig. 1).

ASSEMBLING THE SOAPDISH

3 Cut a 25 cm (10 in) length of 2.5 mm wire. Bend it into the stand section using the template as a guide. Temporarily bind it in place onto the straight section at the bottom of the backbone (fig. 2). Join the length of 1 mm tinned copper wire onto the backbone section immediately below one of the loops at one end with three or four turns. Apply continuous binding along the length of the backbone, removing each temporary binding as you come to it and tying in the ribs and the stand section as you bind. Finish off with two or three turns beneath the loop at the other end of the backbone wire.

fig. 2

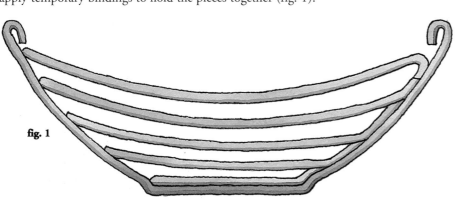

fig. 1

TOPIARY FRAME

Most topiary frames are designed to be used outdoors for large plants, but this one is designed for indoor use with climbing plants such as ivy. The design is inspired by instruments used by seventeenth-century astronomers and navigators.

YOU WILL NEED:

Approximately 14 m (46 ft) of 2.5 mm galvanized wire
Wire cutters or bolt cutters
Approximately 2 m (6 ft 7 in) of 0.8 mm galvanized wire
3 m (9 ft 10 in) of 1.6 mm galvanized wire
Vise grips
Straight-nose pliers

MAKING THE CENTRAL CORE WIRE

1 Cut an 89 cm (35 in) length of 2.5 mm galvanized wire. Make two right angle bends – the first 20 cm (8 in) from the end of the wire and the second a further 40 cm (16 in) along the wire. Using fig. 1 as a guide, make a third right angle bend approximately 2.5 cm (1 in) from this point and bend the wire around to make the top circle, which should be about 5 cm (2 in) in diameter. Continue the wire around for 1½ turns, then bend the wire in towards the centre of the circle. Trim off any excess wire 6 mm (¼ in) before it meets the other side of the circle. Bind the end in place with 0.8 mm galvanized wire at the point shown in fig. 1.

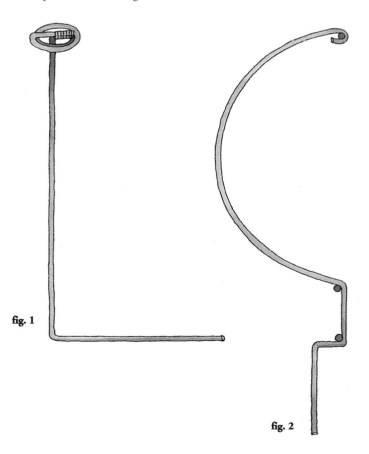

fig. 1

fig. 2

MAKING THE LONGITUDE WIRES

2 Cut sixteen 76 cm (30 in) lengths of 2.5 mm wire. Bend a loop 2.5 cm (1 in) from the end of each wire. Link each wire around the top circle, spacing them evenly. Trim the end of each wire to 6 mm (¼ in) and crimp closed with vise grips.

3 Make a right-angled outwards bend in each longitude wire 48 cm (19 in) from the top circle. Gently bend each longitude wire into a semi-circular curve between the top circle and this right-angled bend (fig. 2). Cut an 18 cm (7 in) length of 2.5 mm wire and form into another 5 cm (2 in) diameter circle. Trim off any excess wire leaving about 1 cm (⅜ in) overlap and bind the ends together with 0.8 mm wire. Thread this circle over the ends of the longitude wires and position it so that it sits in the right angle bend of each length. You can then see if the wires are evenly curved and adjust them as necessary.

4 Cut a 60 cm (24 in) length of 0.8 mm wire and bind the longitude wires, evenly spaced, to the loose circle. Bind the longitude wires to the top circle in the same way.

MAKING THE STAND SECTION

5 The bottom of the central core sticks out horizontally through the straight bottom sections of the longitude wires. Make a right-angled bend in the wire 18 cm (7 in) from the end and bend the wire into a 5 cm (2 in) diameter circle around the outside of all the longitude wires, with the end overlapping by 1 cm (⅜ in). Bend all the longitude wires outwards below the point where they meet this circle. Bend every fourth wire downwards at a further point, 5 cm (2 in) away from the circle and trim the remaining wires just after the point where they touch the second circle. Cut a 60 cm (24 in) length of 0.8 mm wire and bind each longitude wire to the bottom circle (fig. 2).

MAKING THE EQUATORIAL WIRES

6 Cut two lengths of 1.6 mm wire long enough to fit around the circumference of the sphere with about 5 cm (2 in) of overlap. Bend linking loops on the ends of these equatorial wires, trying to gauge the point where you bend the loops so that each wire is an exact fit around the sphere. Position one wire in place around the sphere and temporarily bind it to every other longitude wire. Temporarily bind the second length in place parallel to the first one. Bind the two wires in position with 0.8 mm wire – each length binds the lower equatorial wire where it crosses a longitude wire, then spirals up the longitude wire to bind the upper wire in position.

TIN CAN LANTERN

This decorative lantern is made almost entirely from recycled materials – a tin can cut into sections and a jam jar form the main sections. These are held together with copper wire salvaged from electrical cable. The handle is made from a coathanger, and the can sections are wrapped in copper foil (the only non-recycled part). Most jam jars are slightly too large to fit a regular size tin can, but fortunately for avid recyclers, several brands of pasta sauce come in jars that are a perfect fit. You may find that there is insufficient air for some candles to burn inside the jam jar, but nightlight candles are ideal.

YOU WILL NEED:

Tin can
Protective leather gloves
Heavy duty craft knife
Sheet of paper
Ball-point pen
Copper foil
Scissors
Adhesive tape
Newspaper
Jam jar
Approximately 6 m (20 ft) of 1 mm copper wire
Wire cutters
Vise grips
Awl
Scrap piece of 2.5 x 5 cm (1 x 2 in) wood
Coathanger

CUTTING THE TIN CAN

1 Cutting a tin can is easier than you might think, but do wear a pair of gloves to protect your hands. Use the craft knife to cut around the tin can about 2.5 cm (1 in) up from the base. Use the knife with a sawing action (fig. 1). Repeat about 2.5 cm (1 in) below the top of the can, so that you end up with three sections (you only need the top and bottom sections).

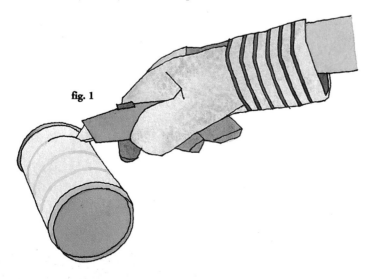

fig. 1

CUTTING THE COPPER FOIL

2 Make six copies of the motif on page 75. Cut a strip of paper and wrap it around the can. The strip should be cut at the point where it overlaps around the can. Fold the strip of paper into six equal parts, then cut out the six motifs and stick one in the centre of each section. Then, cut two strips of copper foil to 5 mm (³⁄₁₆ in) longer than the strip of paper and 2 cm (¾ in) wider than the strip to fit around the outside of the can sections.

3 Tape the foil temporarily in place around each section of the tin can and cut a series of tabs along the top and bottom edges. Remove the foil and lay it on newspaper. Using the ball-point pen, impress the motifs into the foil. Cut another two strips of foil to fit around the inside of each of the two can sections and cut a disc of foil to fit in the base. Position all the pieces and fold over the tabs to lock in place (fig. 2).

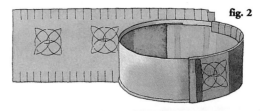

fig. 2

4 Make two small holes between each of the six motifs with an awl (see fig. 3). You may need to place a scrap piece of wood behind the can to support the metal as the hole is made.

POSITIONING THE JAR

5 Cut six 30 cm (12 in) lengths of 1 mm copper wire and fold each one in half. Thread the ends of each length through the pairs of holes around the bottom section of the can (fig. 3).

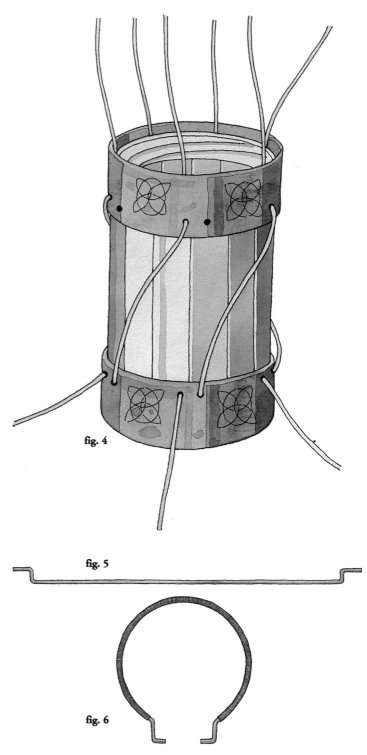

fig. 4

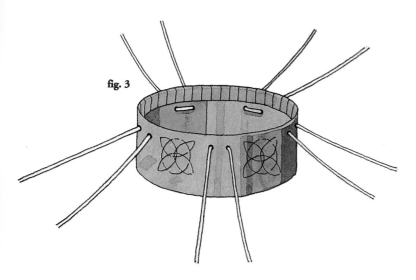

fig. 3

6 Place the jar in position inside the lower section of the can and place the upper can section around the top of the jar.

7 Thread the right-hand ends of the doubled wire sections through the left hand hole two holes to the right in the upper section, then thread the left-hand ends through the corresponding holes two places to the left (fig. 4). Use vise grips to pull each wire tight when they are all in position.

8 You will probably now have a neat pattern of wires over the outside of the jar, and a tangle of ends coming out of the top section. To lock the ends off, twist the wires together in pairs. Trim off any excess wire below the level of the top of the can and press the twisted ends down so that they lie flat.

9 Make two holes for the handle in the upper can section just above the top of the jar. Cut a piece of wire about 35 cm (14 in) long from the straight section of a wire coat hanger. Bend the wire downwards in a sharp right-angle about 2.5 cm (1 in) from each end. Make another bend 5 cm (2 in) from each end, this time upwards (fig. 5). Bring the ends towards each other in a downward arc, so that the centre section of the wire curves gently (see fig. 6).

fig. 5

fig. 6

10 Trim the ends back to 1 cm (⅜ in) before the first right-angle. Bend the arc so that the ends are closer together than the diameter of the tin can which should allow you to snap the ends into position in the holes. The natural spring of the wire should hold the ends in place. Bind with 1 mm copper wire and fit in position to complete the lantern.

CHANDELIER

This project is the only one in the book not to have a bare metal finish. The rust finish is actually a type of paint which comes in two parts: one part contains iron particles and the other an oxidizing agent. When you apply them both to the surface of the wire, a very thin but permanent layer of rust results. Because the surface of the metal is painted, you can use almost any type of wire – copper, aluminium or annealed steel wire would all be suitable.

YOU WILL NEED:

Approximately 5.1 m (16 ft 6 in) of
    2.5 mm wire (copper, annealed
    steel or aluminium)
Wire cutters
Short lengths of 1 mm wire
    (copper, annealed steel or aluminium)
Round-nose pliers or ring bending pliers
Straight-nose pliers
Length of chain
Patina finishes (available from
        craft shops)
Five bottles
Five lamp wicks
Five brass wick holders

MAKING THE FIVE UPRIGHTS

1 Enlarge the large template on page 76. The template is designed to take bottles with a diameter of about 5 cm (2 in); if you wish to use larger bottles, enlarge the template accordingly. Cut five 60 cm (24 in) lengths of 2.5 mm wire. Bend four of them into the spiral-ended uprights using the template as a guide. The fifth should have a hanging loop on the top instead of a spiral. Provide a key at the top of each wire just before the top spiral (or hanging loop) by making a series of light indentations with wire cutters. Temporarily bind all five pieces together with a length of 1 mm wire (fig. 1).

fig. 1

MAKING THE CIRCULAR HOLDERS

2 Cut a 2.1 m (6 ft 11 in) length of 2.5 mm wire. Bend it into a keyring-style double circle (see outer ring of template and fig. 2). Trim off excess wire and bind the ends in place with 1 mm wire. The inner circle and the five small circles are bent from one piece of wire. Bend this with a pair of round-nose or ring bending pliers following the template (see fig. 2). Use wire cutters to make a series of light indentations where the ends join and bind the ends together with 1 mm wire. Trim off any excess wire. Temporarily bind the small circles to the outer circle where they touch.

PUTTING THE CHANDELIER TOGETHER

3 Stand the five uprights on a flat surface (I did this stage on a mat as the wires slipped around and wouldn't stay in position on a smooth surface). Place the inner and outer circles in position over the five uprights. Permanently bind each upright in place where it touches the inner and outer circle. You will notice that there is a slight step on each upright just before it bends round into the 'bowl' shape. After it is tightly bound in place, this step should ensure that each upright will lock in position on the inner circle. Remove the temporary bindings from each area as you add the permanent ones, and pull the permanent bindings tight with a pair of straight-nose pliers.

4 Add 1 mm diameter support wires between the inner and outer circles using the template as a guide. Add 'bowl' shaped support wires running laterally under the position where each bottle will be held, linking around the bottom of the bowl section of each upright wire. These wires start and end off with just a couple of turns around the wires to which they are linked.

5 Remove the temporary bindings that join the five uprights together, just below the top spiral, and replace them with permanent bindings, pulling the wire tight with a pair of straight-nose pliers. Join the length of chain onto the top loop – you can either buy a linking ring with the chain or make a simple circle of 2.5 mm wire – although this circle should be made of steel rather than any other metal as the weight of the whole chandelier will be suspended from it.

6 Apply the patina finish to the chandelier, following the manufacturer's guidelines. Leave to dry, then fill the bottles with oil, add wicks and wick holders and fit the bottles in place.

fig. 2

*Firefly table lamp
(Sophie Jonas)*

*Acorn table lamp
(Phil Medhurst)*

LAMPS & LIGHTS

Red pepper accent lamp
(Sophie Jonas)

Chickenwire and bead lamp
(Willie Simpiwe,
Pan African Market)

5 Starting at one of the arms of the cross-shaped cardboard guide, mark sixteen equal divisions around each circle using the template as a guide. Don't worry if some of the division points are underneath pieces of masking tape – mark the lines on the tape. Check by eye that the marks on all three circles are in line with each other. Gently impress each mark by making an indentation in the wire with the wirecutters.

BINDING THE FRAME TOGETHER

6 Remove one of the small guides and the masking tape either side of it. You should now see three sets of indentations (not counting those immediately next to the ends of the cross-shaped guide). You need to form a wire triangle joining the three circles at each of these three points. Cut a 15 cm (6 in) length of 1 mm galvanized wire. This is longer than you need, but it's easier to grip the wire and bind it tightly when you have a reasonable length of wire to hold.

7 Bind the end of the wire around the outside circle two or three times at one of the indentations. Don't trim the end off at this stage, but carry the wire on to the indentations on each of the inner circles, wrapping the wire twice around each one before continuing the wire back to where it started on the outer circle. Finish by wrapping the wire around two or three times and trim the ends back neatly (fig. 2). If you have very good wire cutters, you may be able to cut the ends off where they touch the outer circle; otherwise trim the ends as close to the outer circle as you can and crimp the end into place with straight-nose pliers.

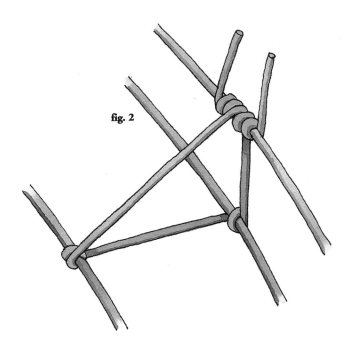

fig. 2

8 When all three triangles are complete, remove the next small guide and repeat the process. When all four sets of three triangles are complete, remove the cross-shaped guide (you may need to cut the cardboard to do this).

9 With a 10 cm (4 in) length of wire, bind the end once around the outer wire at one of the four remaining points. Trim the end so that it sits neatly against the outer circle and cut the wire off 7.5 cm (3 in) from this point. This wire will form one of the four location wires which hold the picture in place. Repeat at each remaining point on the outer wire. Now

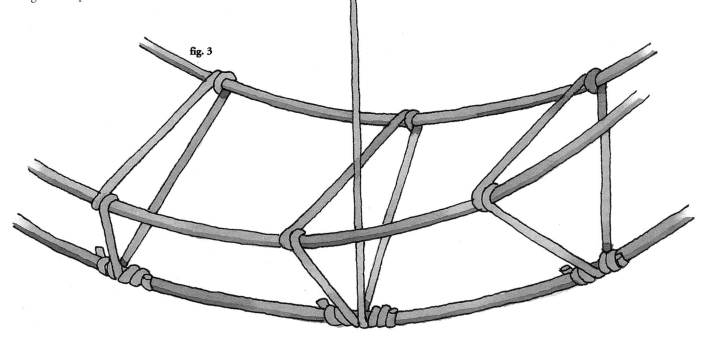

fig. 3

construct a wire triangle at each of these points – these are constructed exactly as before except that the wire starts and finishes either side of the point where one of the location wires is fixed (fig. 3). Apply a small touch of glue at each point around the outer wire where one of the triangles is located.

MAKING THE STAND AND RETAINER

10 Cut two lengths of 1.6 mm wire, one 70 cm (28 in) long for the stand itself and another 52 cm (21 in) long for the stand retainer. Using the templates on page 72 and fig. 4 as a guide, mark the centre point of each piece of wire. Bend the retainer first – this has a simple open loop at each corner, bent about 4 cm (1⅝ in) from the centre point. About 16 cm (6¼ in) from each corner, form a loop on each end that will lock onto the outside circle of the frame. Trim off any excess wire.

11 The stand itself is formed in the same way, using fig. 4 as a guide. This time allow about 21 cm (8¼ in) from the corners to the loops on the ends. It's worth making each loop slightly oversize so that the two stand sections can pivot freely. Position the loops of the the two stand sections on the outer circle and close the loops with a pair of vise grips.

FITTING THE PICTURES

12 Stick your two pictures back-to-back with paper glue. Cut out two discs from the acetate sheet – either use the template as a guide, or use a compass or circle cutter. The discs are about 11.5 cm (4½ in) in diameter. Lay the two circles one on top of the other and mark the positions for the four eyelets. Make a hole at each point with a hole punch. Place the pictures between the two circles and use an eyelet tool to crimp an eyelet into each of the four holes.

13 Hold the completed picture-disc in place in the centre of the frame. Bend the end of each location wire at a right angle so that it will slot neatly in place through an eyelet (fig. 5). To avoid being left with a sharp end, bend the end of each wire back on itself at a point about 1 cm (½ in) from the eyelet. Trim the wire back to about 2 mm (1/16 in).

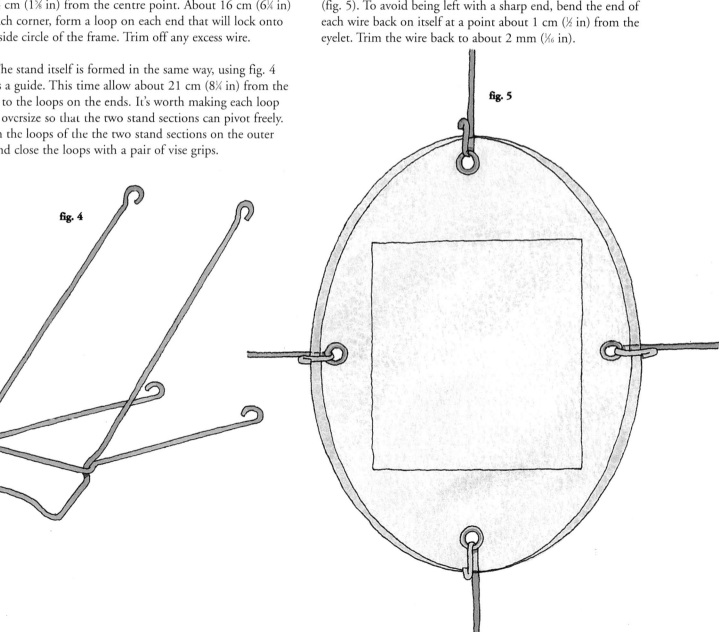

fig. 4

fig. 5

TOASTER

This toaster is similar to a toasting fork except that the toast is gripped between a pair of patterned tongs. The main point of these is to hold your toast firmly (unlike a toasting fork) but they also leave an interesting decorative pattern on the toast. The handle will become hot during use, so wear oven gloves.

YOU WILL NEED:

Approximately 4 m (3 ft 1 in) of 2.5 mm
   galvanized wire
OHP pen
Ring bending pliers
Vise grips
0.25 mm annealed mild steel wire
Flux and a brush
Solder
Soldering iron
Sandpaper
1.6 mm galvanized wire
Bolt cutters

BENDING THE TONGS

1 Enlarge the templates on page 73. Cut two 183 cm (72 in) lengths of 2.5 mm galvanized wire. Straighten them out and mark the centre point on each one with an OHP pen. Take one piece and bend a sharp 'V' bend at the centre point, then follow the curves of the template until you reach the straight section. Now, using ring bending pliers, bend the ends outwards at an angle of 90 degrees. Mark a point 4 cm (1⅝ in) along from the right-angle on each side and double the wire back on itself. Close the bends with vise grips. A further 4 cm (1½ in) on, bend each wire at a right-angle again so that the two wires sit next to one another to form the straight section of the handle (fig. 1). Repeat this process for the second wire.

SOLDERING THE SECTIONS TOGETHER

2 Lay the two sections of wire on top of each other. If necessary, straighten out any kinks so that they match as closely as possible. Mark a point 23 cm (9 in) from the top of the straight section. Temporarily bind the two sections together with 0.25 mm mild steel wire. Apply flux and solder the two pairs of wires together. Allow to cool, then file off any excess solder with a piece of sandpaper and use bolt cutters or a file to provide a key in preparation for binding.

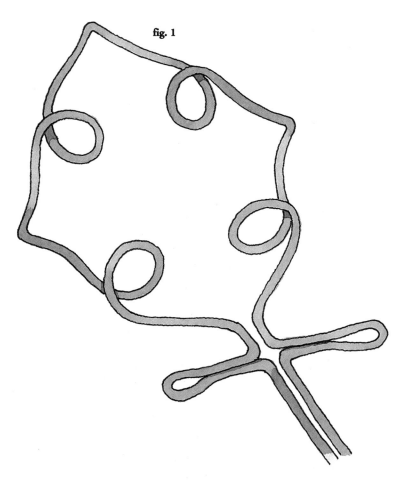

fig. 1

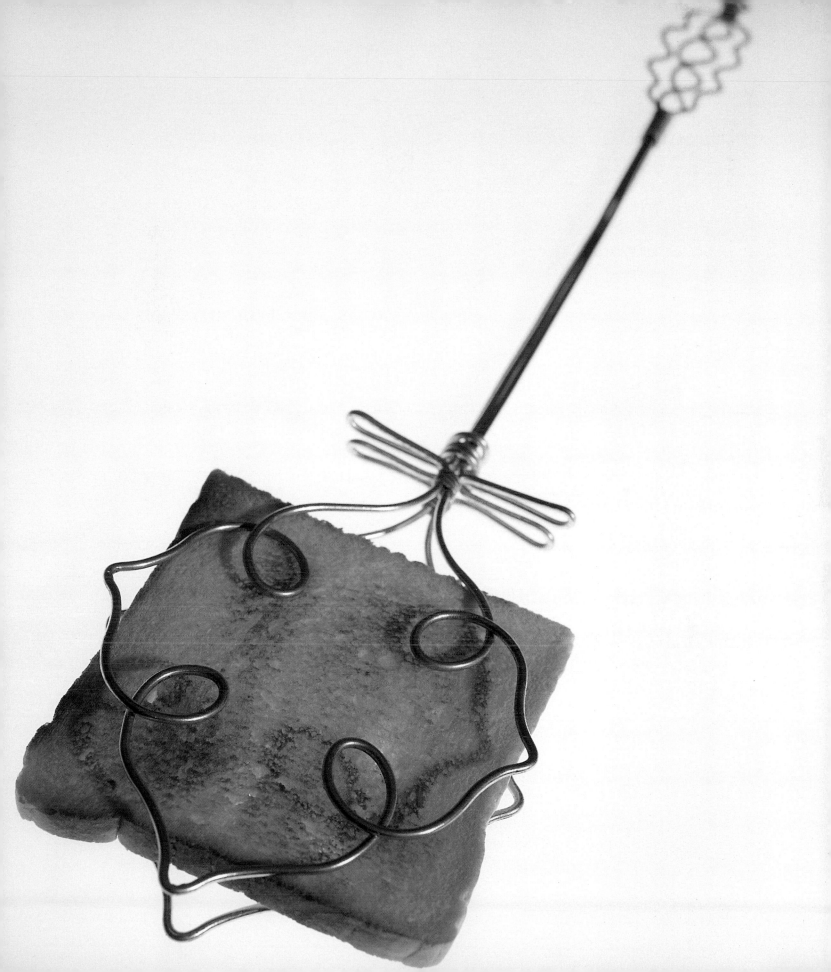

MAKING THE HANDLE

3 Using the template as a guide, bend the wavy section at the base of the handle. The two outside wires follow a simple wavy line, while the innermost pair weave under and over each other (fig. 2). Cut three of the four ends off leaving 1 cm (⅜ in) at the base of the handle. Bend the fourth wire into a loop and cut the end. Key the area above the loop before temporarily binding the wires in place with 0.25 mm wire and then solder together at the point marked with a star.

fig. 2

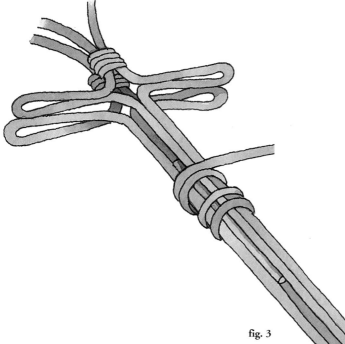

fig. 3

FINISHING OFF

4 Remove all the temporary binding wire and bind over the soldered areas with 1.2 mm wire. Wrap a few turns of 1.2 mm wire around each pair of wires at the base of the toast-gripping section to keep the wires together.

5 Temporarily bind two straight 10 cm (4 in) offcuts of 2.5 mm wire to the straight section (fig. 3). These offcuts serve to increase the diameter of the straight section while you're making the slider – when they are removed, the slider will move freely.

6 To make the slider for the handle, cut a 60 cm (24 in) length of 2.5 mm wire (this is much longer than you'll need, but the extra length gives added leverage and makes the wire easier to bend). Bend three or four loops around the handle and the two offcuts, then cut off any excess wire and slide out the two offcuts. Bend the straight sections so that they gently slope apart from one another, then slope them towards each other towards the end of the toast section.

GARDENING BASKET

This basket uses twigs bound together with wire. The technique is similar to the way that traditional coppice fencing is joined. I've used hazel twigs which are quite common where I live, but any straight-growing wood will work well.

YOU WILL NEED:

Approximately 5 m (16 ft 5 in) of 2.5 mm galvanized wire
Wire cutters
Approximately 8 m (26 ft 3 in) of 0.8 mm galvanized wire
1 sq m (9 sq ft) galvanized wire mesh
Permanent marker
2 large screw hooks
Approximately 50 cm (20 in) length of timber
Approximately 25 straight twigs, each about 30 cm (12 in) long
Round-nose or ring bending pliers
Vise grips

MAKING THE SIDES

1 Enlarge the template on page 77. Cut a 92 cm (36 in) length of 2.5 mm wire and bend the central double-elipse shape of the gardening basket using the template as a guide. Cut a 140 cm (55 in) length of 2.5 mm wire and bend the outer wire, including the handle section (bend the two ends over at the point marked by the arrows). Cut off any excess wire. The points where the wires join are shown on the template: provide a 'key' at each one of these points by making a series of light indentations with a pair of wire cutters. Bind the wires together with a length of 0.8 mm wire and trim off the ends neatly. Repeat this step to make the other side of the basket.

2 Lay each side over a sheet of wire mesh – I've used square mesh with a gap of about 2.5 cm (1 in) between the wires, but any mesh will do. Use a permanent marker to mark around the side, allowing 1 cm (⅜ in) all the way around. Cut the mesh with wire cutters and bend the ends of the mesh over the outer wire of each side to lock it in position. Trim off any excess wire and ensure that each end is tucked in neatly.

MAKING THE BOUND-TWIG BASE

3 The measurements given for the twigs are oversize as it is easier to make the base with 4 cm (1⅝ in) of extra wood on either side, then trim the twigs back when you've finished. Screw the two screw hooks 22 cm (8¾ in) apart into the length of timber. Then either screw the timber to the wall or put the wood face up on the floor and put one foot on either side to hold it in place.

4 Cut two 152 cm (61 in) lengths of 0.8 mm wire. Mark the centre point of each length of wire and fold each wire over a twig at this centre point, with a 20 cm (8 in) distance between the two lengths of wire. If your twigs are all 30 cm (12 in) long, this is 5 cm (2 in) from either end. Because the wires have been joined on at their centre points, you now have a pair of ends hanging down at each side. Grip the left-hand pair of ends with a pair of vise grips and twist them together. Repeat for the right-hand pair, then place the first twig so that it sits in the pair of screw hooks (see fig. 1).

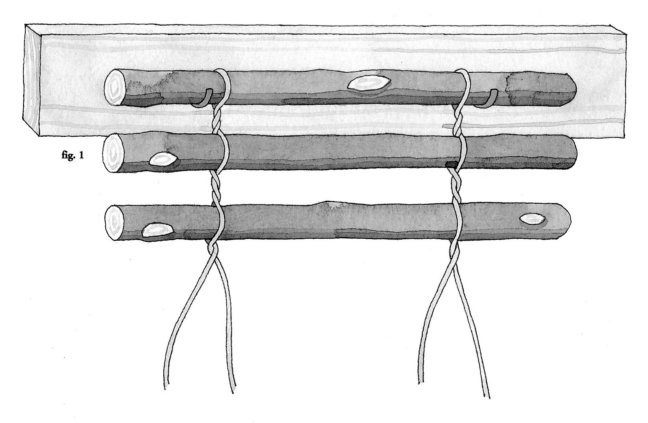

fig. 1

5 Put another twig between the wires and twist as before, although this time twist each pair of wires in the opposite direction. If you turned the vise grips clockwise for the first twist, turn them anti-clockwise this time (see fig. 1). Continue adding twigs and twisting the wires in alternating directions. Check at regular intervals that you are joining the wires on to the twigs 20 cm (8 in) apart from each other. Continue until the 'mat' of twigs fits neatly in place around the outer wire of the sides (it will probably be about 48 cm (19 in) long, but this will vary according to the thickness of the twigs you use).

JOINING THE TWIGS TO THE SIDE SECTIONS

6 Cut a number of short lengths of 0.8 mm wire and use them to temporarily bind the twig mat to the sides. Cut two 76 cm (30 in) lengths of 0.8 mm wire and permanently bind the sides to the base. Begin by binding the end of each wire in place around the outer wire of each side at the point marked on the template with a star. Take each wire all the way around the first twig, then back over the outer wire (fig. 2). Continue working both wires along under each twig and over the outer wire, removing the temporary ties as you go until you get to the end. Bind the end in place around the outer wire and cut off any excess wire. Trim the ends of the twigs back to about 1 cm (⅜ in) away from the line of wires.

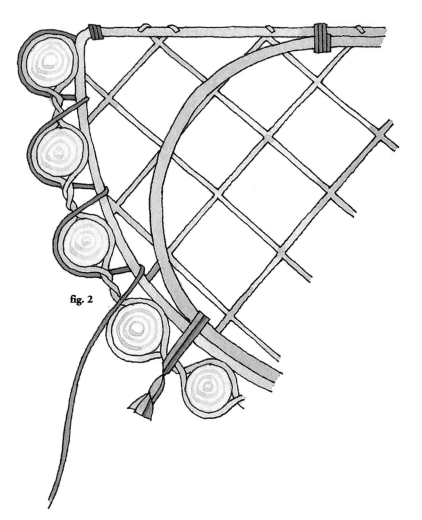

fig. 2

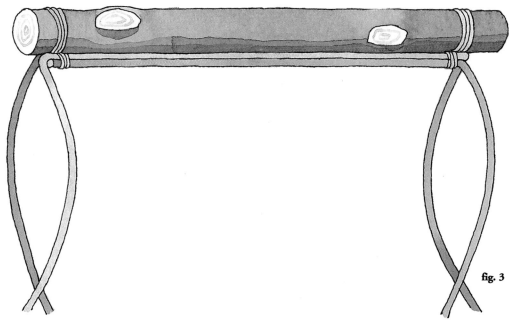

fig. 3

COMPLETING THE HANDLE

7 Pick a relatively thick twig and cut it to 20 cm (8 in) in length. Cut two lengths of 0.8 mm wire and bind them around the handle wires, close to where the horizontal section of the handle meets each of the vertical arms. Take each wire around the twig three times to tie it tightly in position, take another couple of turns around the handle wire and trim off any excess to finish (fig. 3).

KITCHENWARE

1
Condiment holder
(Mia Agnesson)

2
Egg tree
(Combrichon)

3
Utensil rack
(Mia Agnesson)

4
Bookshelf
(Combrichon)

5
Duck egg basket
(Combrichon)

FISH GRILLER

This fish griller is just one one of many things that you could make to cook food over an open fire or barbecue. To ensure the fish doesn't dry out during grilling, wrap it in lightly oiled aluminium foil before you place it inside the fish griller. Most wire becomes softer and more malleable when subjected to heat, and for this reason heavy gauge galvanized wire which will retain its strength has been used for the main framework. If you like the idea of making a fish griller but don't want to spend too much time over it, you could make an alternative version using a wire mesh, such as chicken wire, instead of the woven wires.

YOU WILL NEED:

164 cm (65 in) of 3.5 mm galvanized wire
Wire cutters
Vise grips
104 cm (41 in) of 2 mm galvanized wire
Hammer and anvil
Bolt cutters
Flux and a brush
Solder
Soldering iron
Approximately 5 m (16 ft 5 in) 0.25 mm iron or black
   annealed steel wire
OHP pen
Approximately 6 m (19 ft 8 in) of 1.2 mm galvanized wire
Ring bending pliers

MAKING THE BASE AND LID FRAMEWORKS

1 Enlarge the template on page 78. Make the base framework (which includes the handle) first. Cut a 162 cm (65 in) length of 3.5 mm wire and straighten it. Starting just above the handle, allow 23 cm (9 in) for the straight section then use the template and fig. 1 as a guide to bend the frame of the elliptical shape which will contain your fish.

2 From the base of the elliptical shape, allow 24 cm (9½ in) for the second straight section, then bend the wire outwards at a slight angle at the start of the handle section. Bend a 4 cm (1⅝ in) diameter curve 15 cm (6 in) further on for the rounded end of the handle. Bend a second angle to bring the end back into line with the handle, then trim off any excess wire so that the two ends meet neatly (fig. 1).

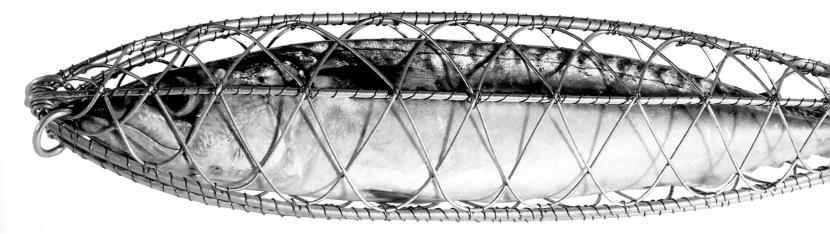

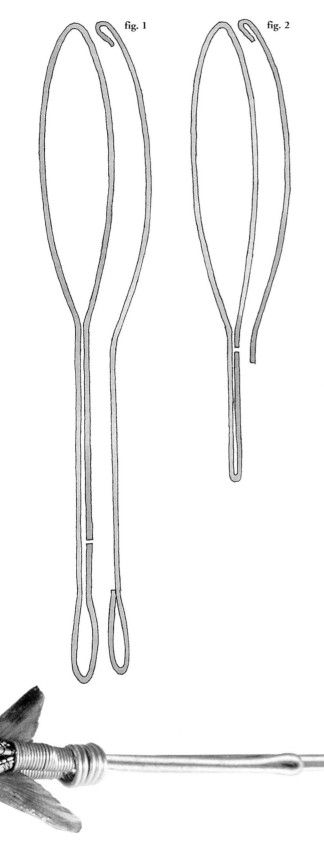

fig. 1   fig. 2

3 The lid framework is made from a 102 cm (40 in) length of 3.5 mm wire with a shorter straight section and no handle. The ends of the lid section meet 1 cm (⅜ in) before the start of the fish container. Follow the template again and take the wire down 13 cm (5¼ in) then bend it back on itself. Use the vise grips to bend the wire round as far as you can, then hammer the bend to complete the recurve (an anvil is the ideal surface to hammer on, but a piece of concrete will also suffice). Trim the ends so the two ends sit together (fig. 2).

THE CENTRAL WIRES

4 To construct the central wire of the base framework, cut a 102 cm (40 in) length of 2.5 mm wire. Straighten it and bend a loop 2.5 cm (1 in) from one end. Following fig. 3, bend a slight angle immediately before the loop so that the wire will lock on to its anchor point at the end of the fish section of the base framework. Using bolt cutters, lightly key the area where the wire will locate before locking the wire loosely in place. Bend a gentle curve in the wire, then a slight angle where it meets the straight section of the base framework. The wire continues right to the end of the handle where it curves back on itself. Trim the end so that it just sits in the 'V' where the handle curves into the straight section.

5 The central piece of the lid section is created in the same way, but is cut off 2 cm (¾ in) after the angle where it joins the straight section.

fig. 3

WASTEPAPER BASKET

I'm very keen to recycle paper rather than just throwing it away, but the base of this wastepaper basket is made from an old tin can so it does have an element of recycling about it! Catering size tin cans can be obtained from cafés and restaurants. Much larger cans are also available, such as those used for vegetable oil. Tin snips, which are available in straight and curved varieties, are useful for cutting large sheets of tin.

YOU WILL NEED:

Catering size tin can or large vegetable oil can
Tape measure
Ruler
Strip of paper
Pencil
Approximately 10 m (32 ft 10 in) of 2 mm tinned copper wire
Wire cutters
Round-nose pliers
Masking tape
Can opener or tin snips
Soldering iron
Solder
Flux and a brush

CUTTING AND BENDING THE WIRE

1 Wash and dry the empty tin can. To measure the circumference of the can, use a tape measure or wrap a strip of paper around it, mark the point where the paper overlaps itself, then measure the length of the piece of paper. Enlarge the template on page 77 so that it is one quarter of the length of the paper strip and make four copies. Stick the four pieces in place around the can with masking tape.

2 Cut 24 pieces of wire, each 28 cm (11 in) long for the upright wires. Following the template, bend these wires with their oval-shaped tops, using round-nose pliers where necessary. Trim off any excess wire. Stick each upright to the template with masking tape. Trim off any excess that protrudes below the base of the can, leaving three uprights with about 1 cm (⅜ in) left below the bottom of the template, equally spaced around the can (one longer wire every eighth wire).

3 For the two horizontal wire circles, cut two pieces of wire 5 cm (2 in) longer than the circumference of the tin can and bend into two circles. Stick each piece in position with masking tape over the top of the row of upright wires.

SOLDERING THE WIRES

4 Flux each point where the upright wires touch the two circles. Carefully solder each join (if a solder joint looks messy, wipe with a damp cloth, apply flux and heat with the soldering iron to re-melt the solder). Try to ensure that each oval shape is soldered closed. When all the joins are neatly soldered, remove the paper template from the tin can.

5 Bring the ends of the circles together so that they will fit together neatly. Temporarily bind the ends of the circles together with two bindings for each joint, leaving room between for the soldering. Solder the overlapped ends together, remove the bindings and trim off the excess wire.

ATTACHING THE SIDES TO THE BASE

6 Cut off the base of the can with a can opener or tin snips. Be sure to cut it so that you include the metal rim with the base. Bend the bottom end of every fourth wire along from one of the longer wires inwards. These three wires will sit on the inside of the rim. Bend the other bottom ends of the uprights outwards so that they will fit outside the rim around the base. Bend the ends of the three oversize wires over so that they tuck underneath the can base and lock the whole structure together (fig. 1). Wash in warm soapy water to remove any traces of flux.

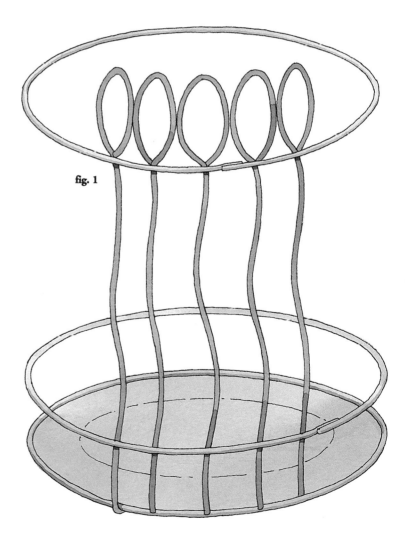

fig. 1

GARDEN & CONSERVATORY

1
Mitre topiary frame
(Rayment Wirework)

2
Wire and chickenwire shoe
*(Winston Rangwani,
Pan African Market)*

3
Traditional bird cage
(maker unknown)

4
Fish griller
(Combrichon)

5
Bee
*(Joe Radebe, Pan
African Market)*

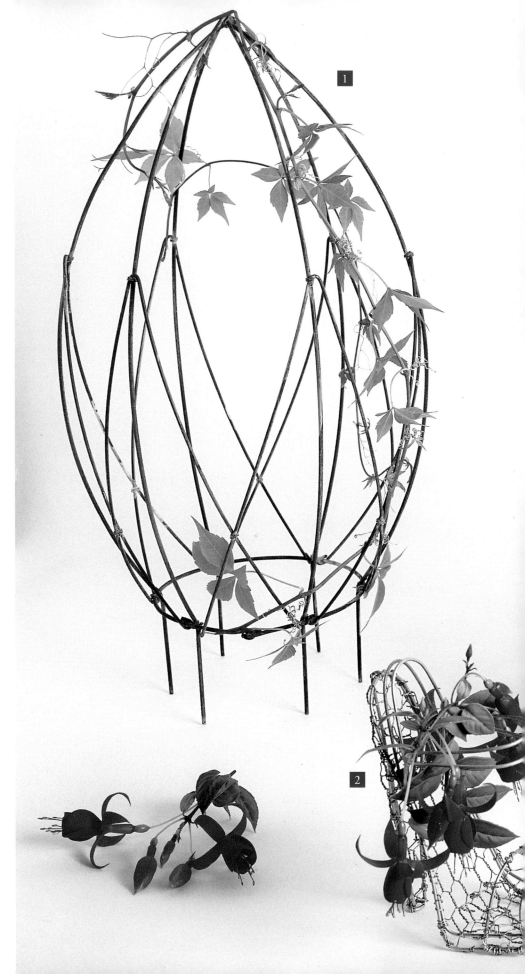

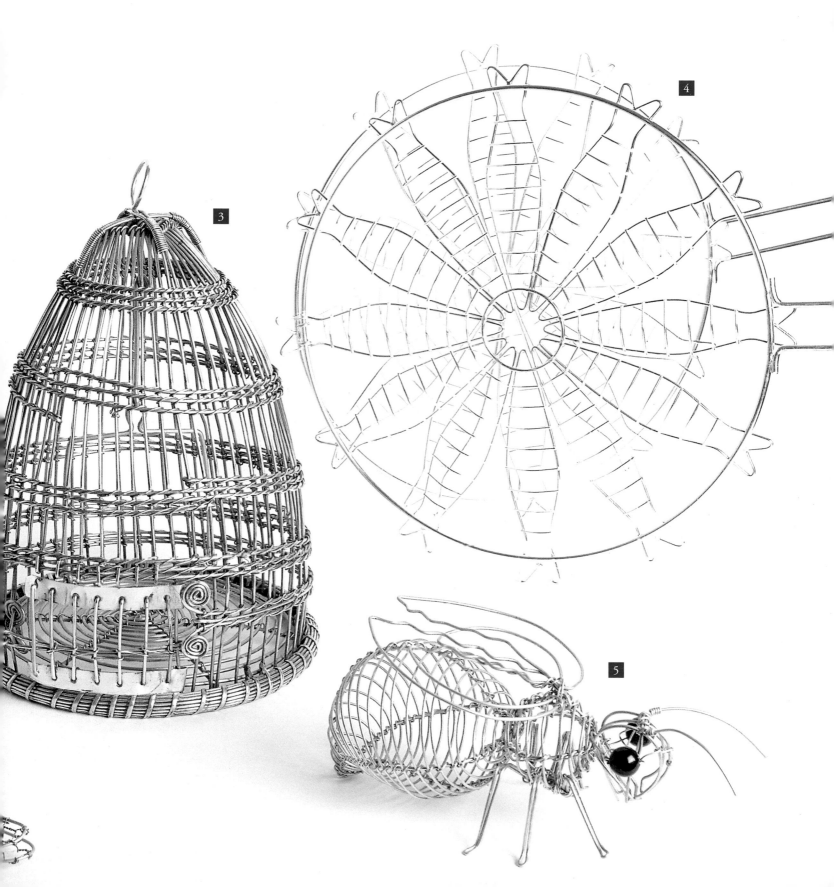

PLANTER

This planter is designed to be freestanding. I've chosen to solder the wires where they meet at the central point, but if you don't fancy soldering, you could bind the wires, or even weave a wire through the uprights to give the structure strength. The base section is constructed as a separate piece, so if you wish to turn the design into a hanging basket all you have to do is leave off the base, add hanging loops around the top circle and attach lengths of chain to the sides. Line the base of the planter prior to planting so that it will hold moisture.

YOU WILL NEED:

Approximately 63 cm (25 in) of 2.5 mm
  galvanized wire
Wire cutters
Vise grips
Approximately 7.5 m (24 ft 7 in) of 1.6 mm
  galvanized wire
OHP pen
Masking tape
30 cm (12 in) of 0.6 mm black annealed steel wire
Soldering iron
Solder
Flux and a brush
Approximately 4 m (13 ft 1 in) of 0.8 mm
  galvanized wire
Straight-nose pliers
Glass bead

FORMING THE TOP CIRCLE

1 Cut a 63 cm (25 in) length of 2.5 mm galvanized wire. Bend it into a circle and bend each end back on itself to form linking loops 2.5 cm (1 in) from each end. Trim the ends back to about 9 mm (⅜ in) and crimp the loops closed with vise grips to form a complete circle.

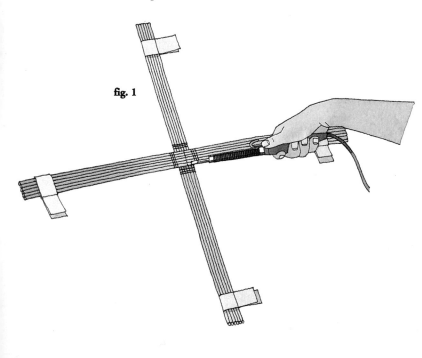

fig. 1

MAKING THE PLANTER UPRIGHTS

2 Cut twelve 44 cm (17½ in) lengths of 1.6 mm galvanized wire. Straighten each wire and mark the centre point on each with an OHP pen. Lay the wires side by side in two groups of six wires, and lay one group over the other to form a cross (see fig. 1). Tape the ends together with masking tape and use a short length of 0.6 mm black annealed steel wire to lightly bind the twelve wires at the centre of the cross.

3 Heat up the soldering iron and place it on the wires at the centre for a minute or two to heat up the wires before applying flux. Melt a pea-sized lump of solder on the end of the soldering iron and hold the iron on the wire until the solder spreads out, bonding the wires together (fig. 1). If the join looks messy, apply more flux and hold the soldering iron on the wire a second time to remelt the solder. When the wire cross is cool, wash it in warm soapy water. Remove the steel binding wire – the solder is unlikely to adhere to this, but if it does, grip one end with vise grips and pull the wire free.

4 Spread out the wires so that they radiate outwards from the centre like the spokes of a wheel. Bend the ends of the wires upwards in a gentle curve. Mark a point 2.5 cm (1 in) from the end of each wire. Bend every sixth end over into a loop at this point, and trim the ends of these four wires back to 6 mm (¼ in). Fit the top circle so that it sits in each of these four loops

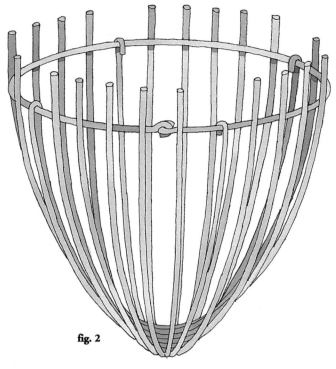

fig. 2

and crimp the four loops closed (fig. 2). Check that each upright wire curves equally.

5 Bend the remaining ends over the top circle, trim the ends back and crimp each loop closed to lock the top circle in place. Cut a 1 m (39 in) length of 0.8 mm galvanized wire and apply a continuous binding around the top circle.

MAKING THE STAND

6 Cut two 29 cm (11½ in) lengths of 1.6 mm galvanized wire and bend each one into a circle. Bend the ends back into linking loops 2.5 cm (1 in) from each end, trim the ends back to 6 mm (¼ in) and crimp the loops closed to complete the two small circles.

7 Cut three 33 cm (13 in) lengths of 1.6 mm galvanized wire and mark the centre point on each wire with an OHP pen. Make another pair of marks on each wire 1.5 cm (⅝ in) either side of the centre mark. Using straight-nose pliers, make a right-angle bend at each of these points to turn each wire into a square 'U' shape. Bend the ends forward into loops 2.5 cm (1 in) from each end, trim the ends back to 6 mm (¼ in) and position the loops around one of the small circles. Crimp the loops closed to lock the wires in place (see fig. 3).

8 Position the second small circle under the bottom of each of the three 'U' shapes and apply a piece of masking tape to hold each one in place. Remove one piece of tape at a time and

apply a continuous binding of 0.8 mm galvanized wire around the circle and the base of each 'U' shape (fig. 3).

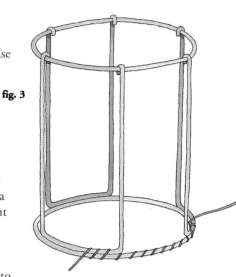

fig. 3

LINKING THE PLANTER AND STAND SECTIONS

9 Stand the completed top section upside down on a worksurface so that the point where the wires are soldered together is uppermost. Cut two 27 cm (10¾ in) lengths of 1.6 mm galvanized wire to form the pair of locking wires which hold the base onto the top section. Mark the centre point on each wire with an OHP pen and thread each one through the planter uprights, just below the point where they are joined together. Bend the ends of each wire upwards (fig. 3).

10 Measure the height of your bead and bend each upright wire slightly outwards from this height upwards (see fig. 4). Place the glass bead between the four wires, press them together and bind them with 0.8 mm galvanized wire (fig. 5).

11 Place the stand structure in place, and bend the ends of the locking wires tightly over the small circle. Trim the ends back to 6 mm (¼ in) and crimp all four ends closed to lock the whole structure together.

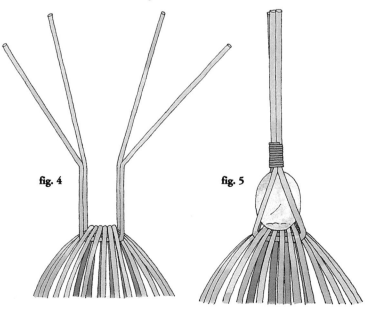

fig. 4

fig. 5

JAPANESE TREE LAMP

The design for the main framework of this lamp was inspired by traditional Japanese lamps. I've used galvanized wire for the framework, but if you find this hard to bend, use tinned copper wire which is softer and can be soldered just as easily.

YOU WILL NEED:

A4 size piece of thick cardboard,
    (210 x 297 mm/8¼ x 11¾ in)
Paper glue
Scissors
Approximately 5.5 m (18 ft 1 in)
    of 2.5 mm galvanized wire
Wire cutters or bolt cutters
Vise grips
Approximately 3.5 m (11 ft 6 in)
    of 1.6 mm galvanized wire
Masking tape
Flux and a brush
Solder
Soldering iron
Strong cardboard box
Freestanding light bulb fitting
OHP pen
Round-nose pliers
Double-sided sticky tape
Sheet of architectural drafting film

MAKING THE FRAME

1 Enlarge the frame template on page 78 and glue it to the sheet of cardboard. Cut four 2.5 cm (1 in) wide strips of thick cardboard and glue one along each side of the rectangle. Cut a 101 cm (40 in) length of 2.5 mm wire and bend it to fit as closely as possible inside the rectangle using a pair of vise grips. Trim off the ends so they meet at one of the corners.

MAKING THE LATTICE

2 Cut two horizontal crossbars to fit between the vertical wires of the rectangle, one from 2.5 mm wire (which will form the lower crossbar) and one from 1.6 mm wire for the central crossbar. Cut four short vertical wires from 1.6 mm wire – these lie across the central crossbar. Tape the rectangular frame and the two crossbars in position on the template with masking tape.

3 Apply flux and solder the ends of the rectangular frame together at the corner. Solder the cross bars to the frame. Leave the wire to cool, then tape the four short vertical wires in position and solder them in place. Leave to cool, then carefully remove the whole framework from the template. Repeat these steps until you have four rectangular wire frames. Bend a kink in the bottom wire (see template) of the side of the frame that will be at the back to allow room for the electrical flex to exit the lamp.

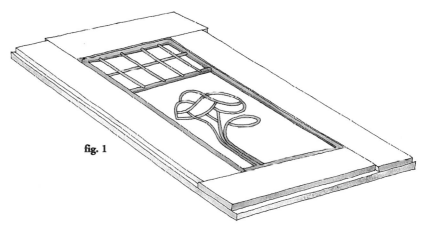

fig. 1

MAKING THE TREE

4 Bend the tree design from 1.6 mm wire using the template as a guide (fig. 1). Tape the pieces to the template and solder them in place. None of the pieces for the tree overlap each other, unlike the pieces for the lattice. The tree is only fixed to the frame where the 'trunk' meets the bottom of the rectangular frame. To ensure that this joint is strong, use more solder than you would for an ordinary solder joint. Remove the frame from the template.

JOINING THE FOUR PANELS

5 To ensure that the rectangular frames meet at a right angle, use a strong cardboard box as a guide. Tape two rectangular frames so that they touch down one edge of the cardboard box and solder them together at the top, the bottom, and at the point where the lower crossbars of the lattice touch (fig. 2). Repeat for the other two sides, then stand the two pairs of sides on a worksurface, tape them together with masking tape to hold them temporarily in position and solder the remaining edges.

ADDING THE LIGHT FITTING

6 To make the light fitting, first enlarge the light fitting template on page 78. Using the template as a guide, bend the circular wire with its four small loops from 1.6 mm wire. Check that this is the correct size for your light bulb fitting by adjusting it from the open end. Ensure that this circle will not be in contact with any metal parts of the lamp fitting – if you are in any doubt, contact a qualified electrician for advice.

7 Cut four 15 cm (6 in) lengths of 1.6 mm wire and make a loop in one end of each wire. Thread these linking wires onto the four loops around the circular wire and tape them to the template. Solder the loops to the circle. Remove from the template and wash the wires in warm soapy water. Fit the circular wire in place on the lamp fitting using the locking ring supplied. Bend the four linking wires downwards at a slight angle (see fig. 3).

8 Stand the lampshade framework centrally over the lamp fitting (fig. 3). Use an OHP pen to mark the point where the framework touches each linking wire. Remove the framework and bend each linking wire sharply upwards at this point. Trim off any excess wire leaving about 6 mm (¼ in) and solder each wire in place to the inside of the framework. Wash the whole framework in warm soapy water and dry it thoroughly.

ATTACHING THE SHADE

9 Lay the framework on its side on a sheet of architectural drafting film and cut a strip that will fit neatly around the whole lampshade. Allow about 5 mm (³⁄₁₆ in) overlap. A thin strip of double-sided adhesive tape down each edge of the framework and along the join in the paper will help to keep it firmly in place.

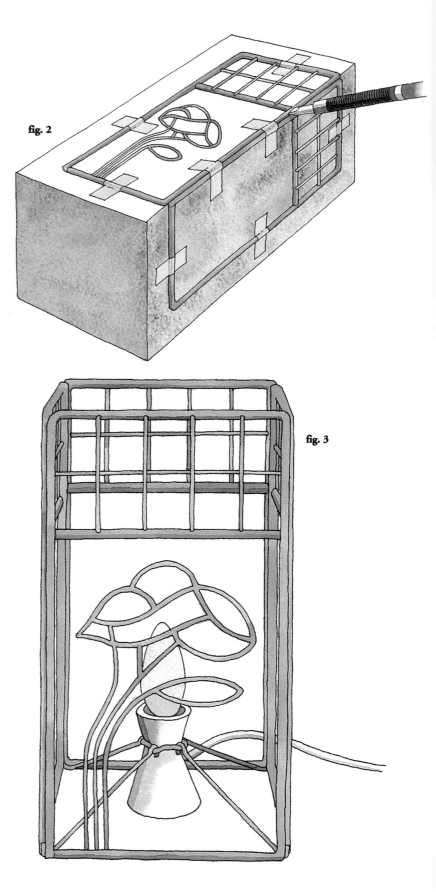

fig. 2

fig. 3

TEMPLATES

Some of these templates are shown smaller than life size. Photocopier enlargement percentages are given where neccessary. 141% is the standard A4 to A3 enlargement.

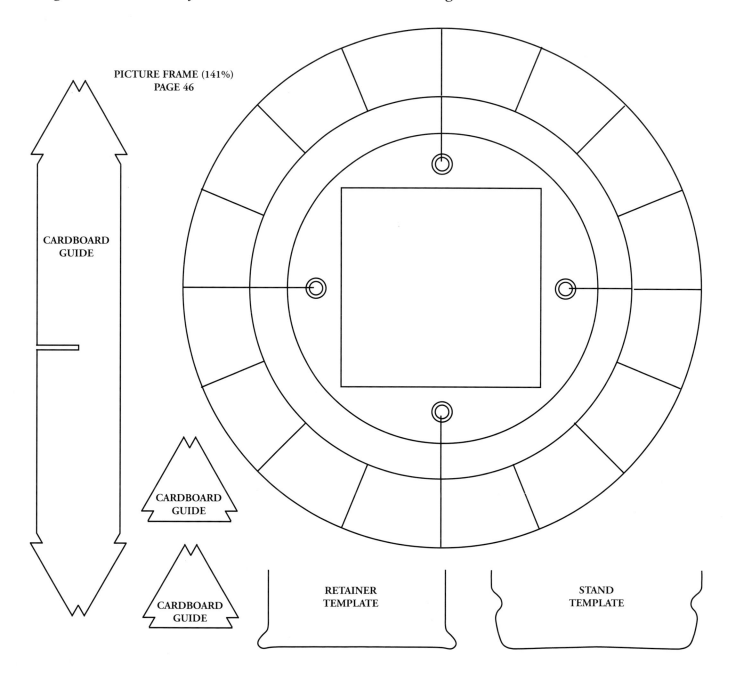

PICTURE FRAME (141%)
PAGE 46

CARDBOARD GUIDE

CARDBOARD GUIDE

CARDBOARD GUIDE

RETAINER TEMPLATE

STAND TEMPLATE

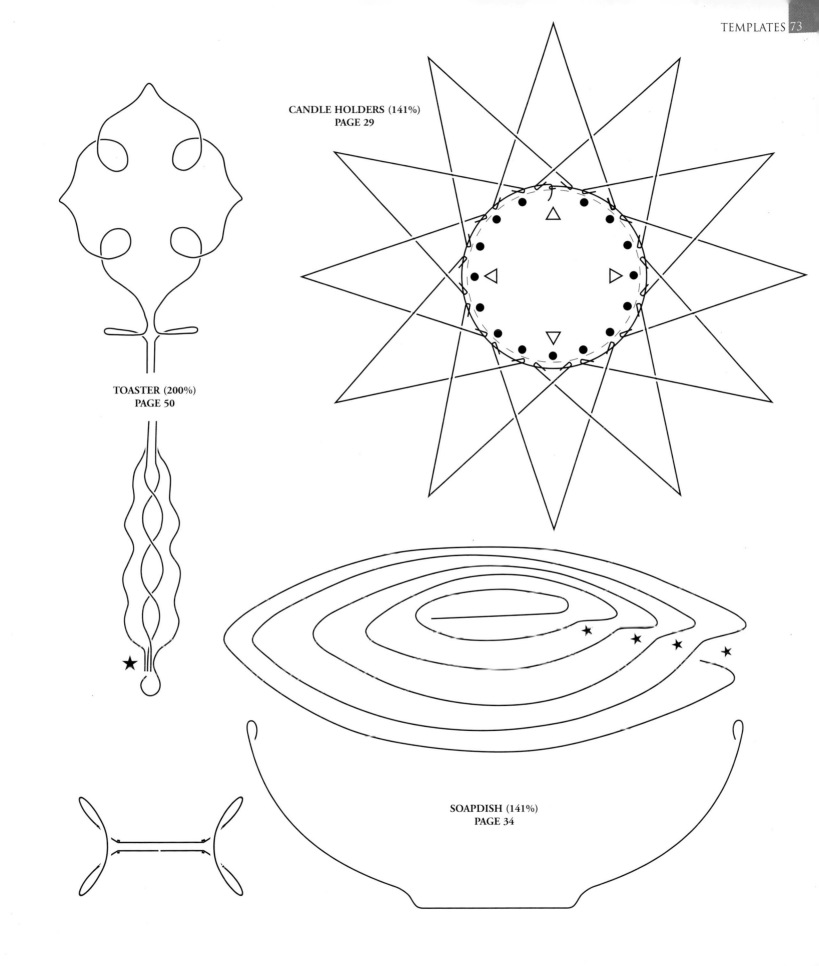

CANDLE HOLDERS (141%)
PAGE 29

TOASTER (200%)
PAGE 50

SOAPDISH (141%)
PAGE 34

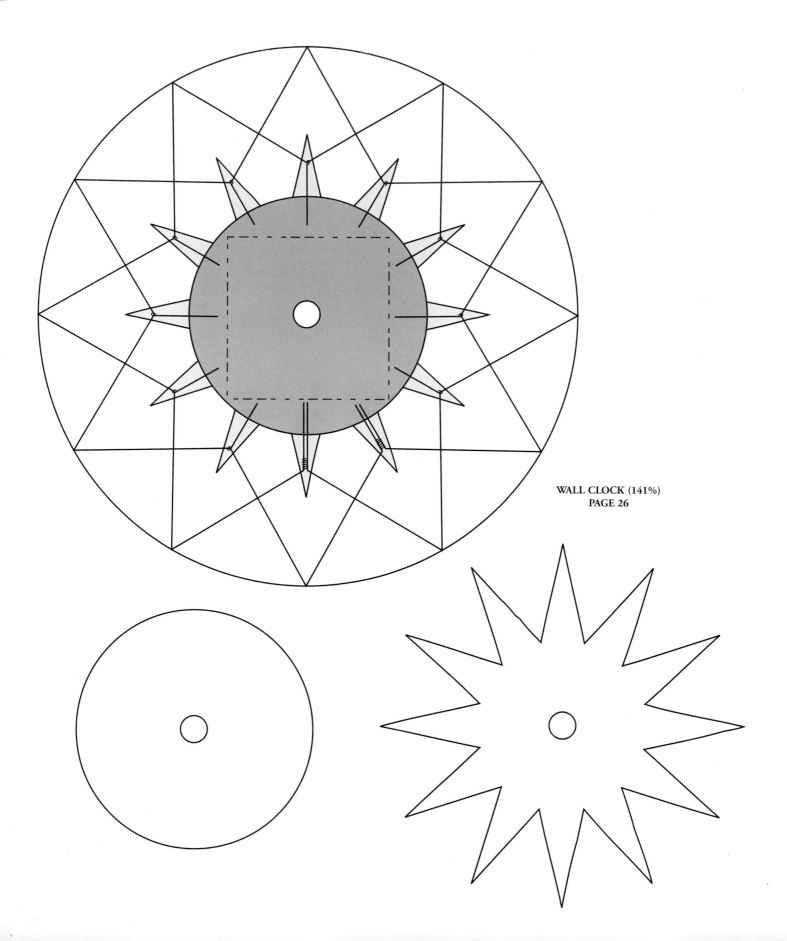

WALL CLOCK (141%)
PAGE 26

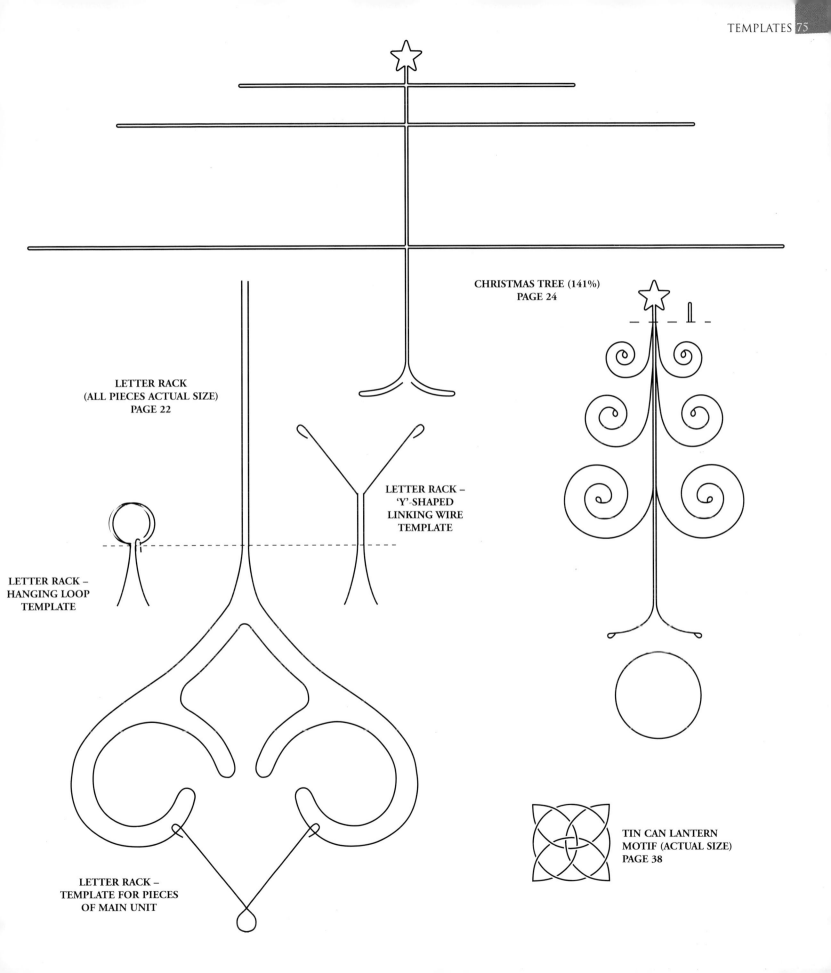

CHRISTMAS TREE (141%)
PAGE 24

LETTER RACK
(ALL PIECES ACTUAL SIZE)
PAGE 22

LETTER RACK –
'Y'-SHAPED
LINKING WIRE
TEMPLATE

LETTER RACK –
HANGING LOOP
TEMPLATE

LETTER RACK –
TEMPLATE FOR PIECES
OF MAIN UNIT

TIN CAN LANTERN
MOTIF (ACTUAL SIZE)
PAGE 38

CHANDELIER (200%)
PAGE 41

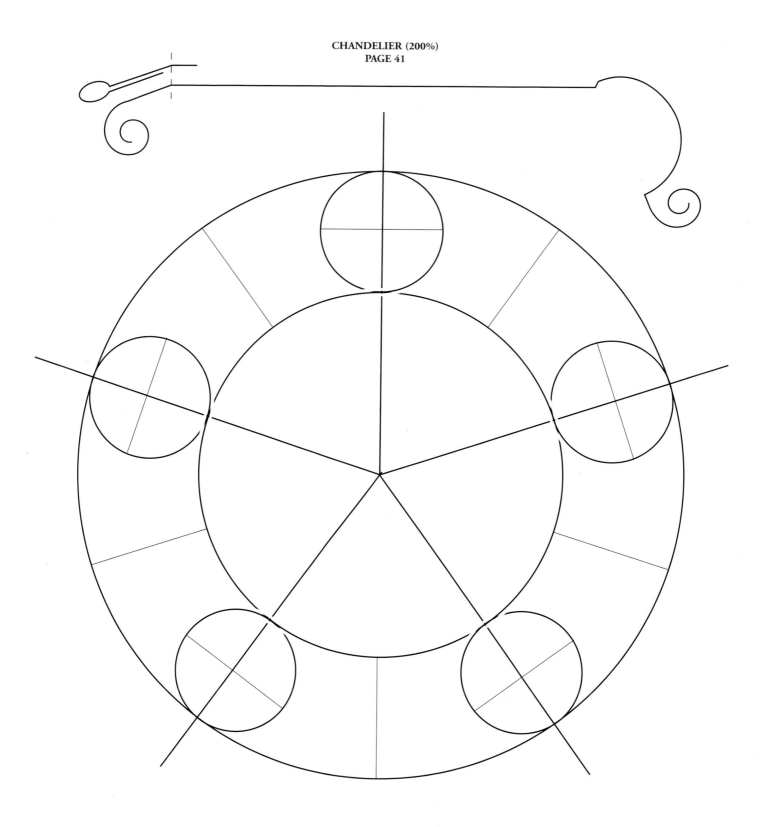

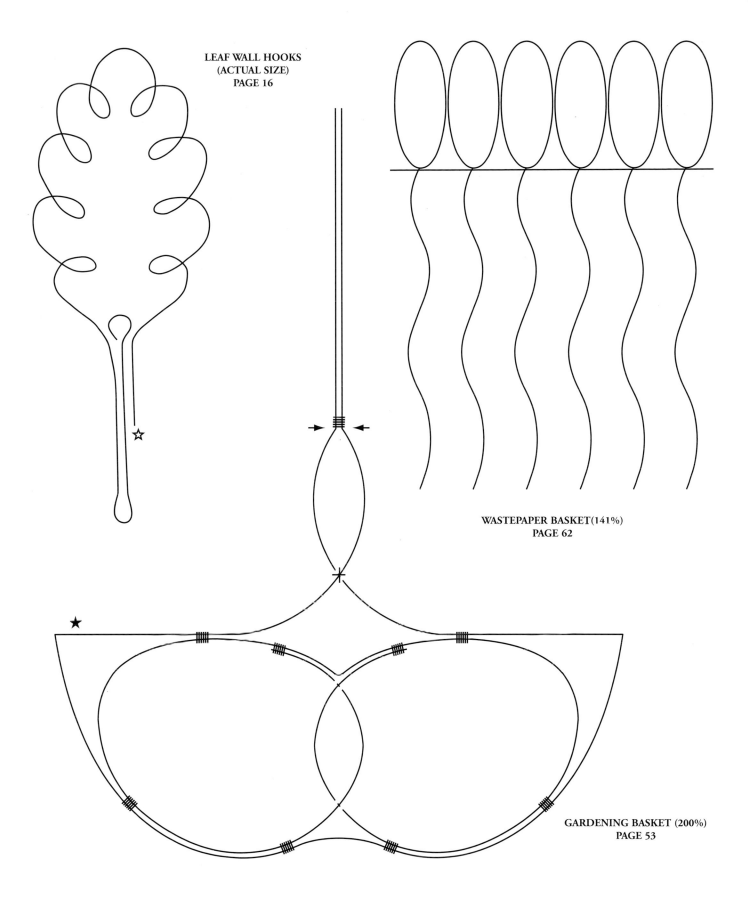

LEAF WALL HOOKS
(ACTUAL SIZE)
PAGE 16

WASTEPAPER BASKET(141%)
PAGE 62

GARDENING BASKET (200%)
PAGE 53

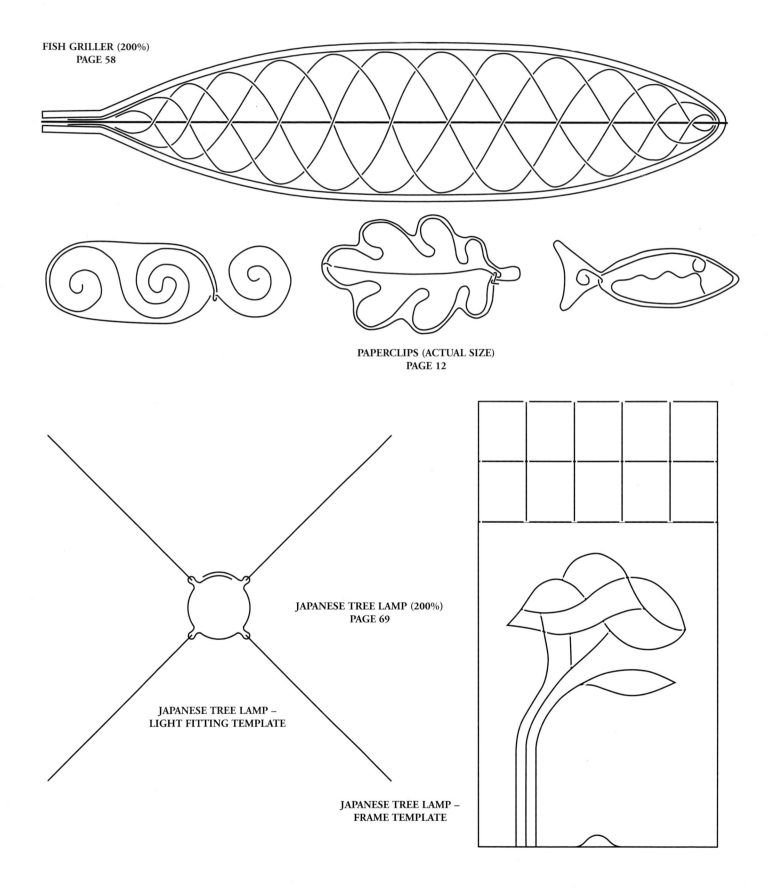

FISH GRILLER (200%)
PAGE 58

PAPERCLIPS (ACTUAL SIZE)
PAGE 12

JAPANESE TREE LAMP (200%)
PAGE 69

JAPANESE TREE LAMP –
LIGHT FITTING TEMPLATE

JAPANESE TREE LAMP –
FRAME TEMPLATE

CONTRIBUTORS

Wendy Abrahams
30 Dale View Crescent
Chingford E4 6PQ
UK
e-mail:
bendywendywoo@hotmail.com

Mia Agnesson
Trad Av Metal
159 Farrell Street
Port Melbourne 3207
Australia
Tel: 613 9645 4227

Alison Bailey Smith
40 Southampton Street
Guelph, Ontario, N1H 5N4
Canada

Combrichon
Usine de Forquevaux
BP12601600
Trevoux, Cedex
France
Tel: 33 474 00 17 38

Tasuku Gouda
Chikusa-ku Kouyou-cho 2-46
Aichi Nagoya
464-0062
Japan

Sophie Jonas
Brook House Design Studios
Blue Bridge Road
Brookmans Park, nr Hatfield
Hertfordshire AL9 7SX, UK
Tel: 01707 656531

Phil Medhurst
56 Pennington Road
Southborough, Kent
UK

Rayment Wirework
Unit 10
Laundry Road
Minster in Thanet
Kent CT12 4HL
UK
Tel: 01843 821628

Idonia Van Der Bijl
25A Museum Street
London WC1A 1JT
UK
Tel: 0171 636 4650

Michael Methven, Willie
Simpiwe, Winston Rangwani, Joe
Radebe and Leroy Lichaba at the
excellent Pan African Market
76 Long Street
Cape Town
South Africa
Tel: 27 21 4242 957
www.panafricanmarket.co.za

SUPPLIERS
UK

APTC
Axminster
Tel: 01297 35554
General tools supplier with good
range of pliers

Art Emboss
Call 020 8888 6888 for details of
your nearest stockist. Soft copper,
brass, pewter and aluminium foil

B & Q Plc branches thoroughout
the country. To find your nearest
branch, contact:
Tel: 0800 444840
General tools supplier

Firecraft Studios – Unit 5
Longmoor Craft Workshops
Cranbury Park
Otterbourne
Winchester SO21 2RH
Tel: 01703 276727
Lamp wicks, colouring mediums
for lamp oils, wick holders, copper
plated annealed steel wire

Lead & Light
35A Hartland Road
London NW1 8DB
Tel: 020 7485 0997
75w and 100w soldering irons,
solder, safety flux, tin sheet

Maidstone Engineering Services
4 Larkstore Park
Lodge Road
Staplehurst
Kent TN12 OQY
Tel: 01580 890066
Mail order metal and
wire suppliers

Scientific Wire Co
18 Raven Road
London E18 1HW
Tel: 020 8505 0002
Large range of different types
of wire

H.S. Walsh
21 St Cross Street
Hatton Garden
London EC1N 8UN
Tel: 020 7242 3711
Ring bending pliers, parallel pliers

US

Wire, pliers and soldering irons
are readily available at most local
hardware and home improvement
stores. Check for the one nearest
you or contact one of the specialty
suppliers listed below.

Paul Gesswein & Co Inc
255 Hancock Avenue
P.O. Box 3998
Bridgeport, CT 06605-0936
Tel: 203 366 5400
Tools supplier with excellent range
of pliers and cutters

Paragona Art Products
1150 18th Street, Suite 200
Santa Monica, CA 90403
Tel: 310 264 1980
Soft copper, brass pewter and
aluminium foil

Studio Design Inc
1761 Route 34 South
Wall, NJ 07727
Tel: 732 681 6003
75 watt and 100 watt soldering
irons, solder and safety flux

Textron Anchor Wire Co.
425B Church Street
Goodlettsville, TN 37072
Tel: 615 859 1306
Black annealed steel wire

SOUTH AFRICA

Federated Timbers (and Feds DIY)
branches throughout the country.
To find your nearest branch,
contact: Johannesburg:
(011) 453-3330

Mica Hardware branches
thoroughout the country. To find
your nearest branch, contact:
Johannesburg: (011) 444-0722
Durban: (031) 563-4400

AUSTRALIA

BBC Hardware
Head Office, Bldg A
Cambridge Street
NSW 2121
Tel: (02) 9876 0888
(outlets nationwide)

Mitre 10
319 George Street
Sydney 2000
Tel: 1800 803 304
(outlets nationwide)

NEW ZEALAND

Spotlight
Head Office
Tel: 09 262 5090